Introduction

When we set out to gather stories f. *Patchwork of Appalachian Christmas Stories*, we weren't just collecting words—we were chasing the echoes of laughter, the smell of wood smoke mingled with pine, and the flickering glow of lights in frosted windows. Appalachia is a place where tradition runs deep, where family ties are as strong as the mountains that cradle the valleys, and where the holiday season brings out a unique blend of ingenuity, resilience, and heart.

Over the past 10 years, we traveled the winding roads and hollers of Virginia, West Virginia, North Carolina, Tennessee, and Kentucky, stopping in small towns and even smaller communities. Our goal was simple: to capture the essence of Christmas as it's celebrated in this remarkable region. What we found, though, was anything but simple.

The stories we gathered were as diverse as the people who shared them. Some told of deeply rooted traditions. Others shared tales of resourcefulness, like turning scraps of wood into toys or foraging the woods for mistletoe to hang above the doorway. There were poignant memories of Christmases, when the simplest gift—a handmade doll, a fresh orange, or even a snowball fight—meant the world.

We also uncovered traditions that could only exist in Appalachia. And, of course, there were the songs—ballads that blend old-world melodies with the spirit of the season, sung by crackling fires or under star-filled skies.

These stories are more than a celebration of Christmas—they're a testament to the Appalachian way of life. They speak of resilience in hard times, joy in simplicity, and the enduring belief that family and community are what truly make the holidays bright.

As we present these tales to you, we hope you'll feel the warmth of the homes we visited and hear the laughter of the storytellers who welcomed us in. These aren't just their stories—they're part of the fabric of Appalachia, threads woven into a rich and enduring tapestry of holiday traditions.

So, pour yourself a cup of cider, curl up under a quilt, and join us on this journey through the hollers and hills of Appalachia. Let the stories in this collection transport you to a place where the magic of Christmas is alive in every corner, where memories are made not just of what we have, but of how we share it.

—Shane Simmons & Melody Blackwell-West

Christmas in the Holler

In the hollers of Appalachia, where the mountains kiss the sky,
Christmas came with whispers soft, as snowflakes floated by.
A cedar tree, so humble, stood in the corner of our home,
Draped with strings of popcorn and tinsel we'd made on our own.

The fire crackled warmly, its glow a golden light,
While Mama hummed sweet carols on a frosty, starlit night.
The scent of pine and wood smoke danced softly through the air,
And though our gifts were simple, love was everywhere.

No shiny store-bought treasures wrapped beneath our tree,
But Daddy's laughter echoed, filling us with glee.
A quilted blanket handmade by Grandma's loving hands,
And jars of home-canned peaches were gifts that met our plans.

The hills would hold their silence as the world lay hushed in snow,
And the holler seemed enchanted in the firelight's gentle glow.
We'd sit and share old stories, of kin who'd gone before,
Their voices still alive to us, though we'd hear them no more.

The church bells in the valley rang out a holy song,
As neighbors gathered warmly, a close and faithful throng.
We'd sing of peace and goodwill, of hope that brightly burns,
Of Christ who came to save us, as the weary world still turns.

No matter how lean the years, or how hard times might be,
We found the joy of Christmas in our mountain family.
For riches weren't in gold or toys beneath the tree,
But in the love that bound us, steadfast and quietly.

So now, when Christmas finds me far from that old mountain home,
I think of snowy hollers, and how far my heart has roamed.
And though the years have scattered us, those memories remain,
Of Christmas in Appalachia, where joy outshined the pain.

The Christmas Horse: A Gift of Kindness in the Snow

I can still smell the pine needles and wood smoke whenever I think about that Christmas, so many years ago in the hills of Kentucky. It was the winter of 1953, and I was just a little girl— almost 8 years old. Christmas was a simpler thing back then. We didn't have much money, but we had the mountains, our family, and a whole lot of hope. I reckon those things are more valuable than anything you can buy at a store.

We lived in a little two-room cabin, nestled in the holler near Jenkins, Kentucky. Pa worked at the coal mines, and Ma kept the house running, which was no small feat with six kids. Life was tough, sure, but us kids didn't know any different. We ran barefoot in the summers and bundled up in the winters, making our fun with whatever we could find—sticks, stones, and stories passed down from the older folks.

That year, though, Christmas felt special in a way that it hadn't before. There was something about the air, crisp and sharp with a cold that made your cheeks red and your breath fog up in little clouds. Ma had been saving flour and sugar for weeks, and I knew she was planning on making her famous apple stack cake. That was a real treat, a cake made with layers and layers of thin dough and apples dried over the fire. It was like a piece of heaven on a plate.

I remember waking up that Christmas Eve with snow coming down in soft, steady flakes. The whole holler was covered in white, and it made the world seem quiet and hushed, like even the trees were holding their breath. Pa had chopped enough wood to keep the fire going all night, and the cabin was warm, filled with the smell of that stack cake baking in the oven.

Now, we didn't have a Christmas tree like you see nowadays in town, all decorated with fancy lights and tinsel. Pa had gone out a few days before with my brothers to cut a small pine tree from the woods. It wasn't perfect, but to us, it was beautiful. Ma let us make decorations from whatever we could find—pieces of old cloth tied into bows, paper chains made from scraps of brown paper sacks, and pinecones dusted with flour to make them look like they were covered in snow. And, of course, the star on top was made from a bit of tin foil Ma had saved from a candy wrapper last year.

That night, we all gathered around the fire after supper, full bellies from a simple meal of ham hock and beans. Pa sat in his old rocking chair, whittling a piece of wood with his pocketknife, while Ma hummed a soft tune, rocking the baby in her lap. My brothers, Johnny and Earl, were working on a puzzle they'd gotten from the schoolteacher last Christmas. My sisters, Ruthie and Sue, were by the tree, whispering secrets and giggling in that way only sisters can.

But I'll never forget what happened next. Just as we were settling in for the night, there was a knock at the door—a strong, steady rap that echoed through the cabin. Now, visitors were few and far between in those days, especially in the middle of winter when the roads were hardly passable. Pa looked up from his chair, his brow furrowing in concern. "Who in the world could that be?" he muttered, setting down his knife and wood.

He walked over to the door and opened it, and standing there in the snow was Old Mr. Wills. He was our nearest neighbor, but that wasn't saying much since he lived about a mile away, up the mountain. He was a widower, probably in his seventies, with no family to speak of. I always thought of him as a quiet, lonely old man, the kind who kept to himself. But there he was, standing in the snow, holding a small bundle wrapped in a brown cloth.

"Well, come on in, Mr. Wills!" Ma said, standing up and moving toward the door. "You must be half frozen!"

Mr. Wills stepped inside, shaking the snow off his boots and unwrapping the bundle in his hands. "I wasn't planning on stayin' long," he said in his gravelly voice. "But I wanted to bring y'all this." He handed the bundle to Pa, and when Pa opened it up, inside was the most beautiful carved wooden toy I had ever seen. It was a horse, perfectly shaped, with a smooth, polished finish. It had real leather reins, and its mane and tail were made of bits of yarn.

I stared at that toy horse with wide eyes, hardly able to believe it. I had never seen anything so fine. Mr. Wills had carved it himself—he was known to be good with his hands, but this was something else. Pa turned it over in his hands, a slow smile spreading across his face.

"Mr. Wills," Pa said, "this is mighty kind of you."

Mr. Wills shrugged, looking down at his boots. "Figured your young'uns might like somethin' for Christmas. Didn't have nobody else to give it to."

I didn't know it at the time, but Ma later told me that Mr. Wills had lost his only son many years before, during the war. After that, he had kept to himself, rarely speaking to anyone. But that night, he had trudged through the snow to bring us that gift. And it wasn't just the horse—it was something much deeper. It was the spirit of Christmas, of kindness and giving without expecting anything in return.

Pa invited him to stay for a while, and though Mr. Wills protested at first, he finally sat down by the fire, and Ma handed him a slice of apple stack cake. We spent that evening listening to Pa tell stories and singing old hymns together, with Mr. Wills sitting quietly in the corner, a faint smile on his face as he watched us.

I remember looking around the room, at the flickering firelight dancing on the walls, at my brothers and sisters laughing and playing, and at Mr. Wills, who had come out of the cold to share a bit of warmth with us. It wasn't a Christmas of fancy presents or store-bought decorations, but it was the best one I've ever had. It was a Christmas filled with love, generosity, and the simple joy of being together.

The next morning, when we woke up, Mr. Wills was gone. Pa said he had left early, probably before dawn, to get back home before the snow got any worse. But that little wooden horse he left behind stayed with us for years. It became a symbol of that Christmas, a reminder that even in the hardest times, there's always room for kindness.

I'm an old woman now, and the world has changed in ways I couldn't have imagined back then. But whenever I think back to that year, I think back to that little cabin in the holler, to the smell of apple stack cake and pine needles, and to the old man who walked through the snow to remind us of the true meaning of Christmas.

Christmas Memories from the Appalachian Mountains: A Boy's Journey Back to 1960s Appalachia

There's a kind of magic to Christmas in the Appalachian Mountains, a quietness in the world that seems to fall in time with the first gentle snow, blanketing the hollers and trails we roamed as kids. I was a boy in the 1960s, raised in the small mountain town of Burnsville, North Carolina, where folks knew each other, looked after each other, and life followed the simple rhythms of the seasons. To this day, I carry those Christmas memories with me like an old, beloved tune, one that comes back to you when you least expect it but always fills your heart.

Christmas was different back then—simple, sure, but in the best ways possible. I remember us kids waiting all year long, counting down the days until the first December snowfall, when my brothers and I would press our noses against the frosted window and watch as the snow coated every tree branch and rooftop. It wasn't Christmas yet, but it was the promise of it, and in those mountains, Christmas felt like it was a part of the land itself.

Come December, my family would pull out the same few strings of lights, tangled and dusty from the year before. Mama would carefully place them around our tree, which we'd go and pick out from the woods just behind our house. We didn't buy trees back then; we'd simply grab an old saw and head out with my Pa, looking for a good-sized spruce that felt just right. He'd hoist it over his shoulder, and I remember thinking he looked just like one of the big men in those old paintings, carrying a piece of the mountain itself right into our living room.

Decorations weren't store-bought; they were hand-made with whatever we could find around us. My sister and I would string together popcorn garlands, carefully poking kernels onto the thread while nibbling a few ourselves. We'd dig out pinecones, maybe dip them in some paint or roll them in salt to make them sparkle, though that was a rare treat. Mama would hang a few red ribbons, and sometimes, if she had extra fabric from her sewing, she'd fashion little bows or even tiny stockings to hang on the tree. That tree might not have looked much to some folks, but to us, it was the grandest thing in the world.

We didn't have much, but Christmas Eve brought a richness to our home. My grandparents would come over, and aunts, uncles, and cousins, too, filling our small house with laughter and warmth. We'd crowd around the fireplace, listening to the crackling wood and swapping stories of past Christmases. My grandpa would tell us about the hard winters of his boyhood, how his family would rely on what little they could grow or trade. Somehow, in hearing about those tougher days, we were reminded how lucky we were, even if we didn't have all the fancy things we saw in magazines or heard about from friends.

I remember we didn't expect much in the way of presents. A few weeks before Christmas, Mama would give us the Sears Roebuck catalog, and we'd thumb through it, picking out a single toy or item that caught our eye, knowing full well we might get it or might not. One year I asked for a cap gun set, convinced that was the finest thing a boy could own. On Christmas morning, there it was, wrapped in brown paper under the tree, and I felt like I'd been given the world.

But even without many presents, Christmas always felt whole. The gifts we gave each other were often made with our hands— homemade candy or a scarf that Mama had stayed up late knitting by the fire. I remember Pa once made me a slingshot from a sturdy branch and an old rubber band, his calloused hands wrapping that rubber around the wood with such care. I think I prized that slingshot more than anything else I've owned since.

One of my favorite memories was the candlelight service at our little church on Christmas Eve. The whole town seemed to turn out, filling the pews with folks in their Sunday best. There was a hush as the pastor spoke, his voice warm and familiar, telling the story of Christ's birth. Each of us held a little candle, and when they were all lit, the church would glow, soft and golden. I remember looking at that flickering light reflected in the faces around me and feeling something deep and pure—a sense of belonging, of love, of something far bigger than myself.

Then we'd sing carols, and I'd look over to my mama, her voice soft but steady, singing "Silent Night" with the kind of reverence that made me feel she understood things I didn't. My dad's rough hand would find mine, squeezing it as if to say, "This is what matters." It was a reminder that, in that small mountain town, on that quiet Christmas Eve, we were exactly where we belonged.

Christmas dinner was a feast by our standards—ham, cornbread, beans, and Mama's sweet potato pie. Every bite felt like a treasure, especially when my cousins and I would sneak a second helping of pie. We knew it wasn't just food; it was family, tradition, a reminder of the hands that had worked hard all year to put it there.

Now, all these years later, when I think back to those Christmases in the Appalachians, it's not the presents I remember most, nor even the tree or decorations. It's the feeling, the warmth of a fire with family gathered around, the songs, the stories, the sense that we were connected to each other and to the land around us. It's a sense of gratitude, of contentment that came from the simple things, things that couldn't be wrapped or bought.

I hope those memories never fade, and I carry them with me each Christmas as I watch my own children and grandchildren celebrate. I realize now that the gifts we were given back then weren't really the ones under the tree but the love and traditions that have carried on through the years. That's the true magic of a mountain Christmas, one that lingers in your heart and brings you home every time you remember.

Remembering a Christmas Without Presents: Memories from the Appalachian Mountains

Christmas has a way of stirring up memories—those bittersweet pieces of the past that stay with us, no matter how much time has gone by. Looking back, I'm reminded of how different Christmas was when I was a boy growing up in the Appalachian Mountains. We didn't have much in the way of money or luxuries, and there were years when even a small gift under the tree was a big ask. One Christmas, in particular, stands out in my mind—one that, though it was filled with love, came with a kind of emptiness I'd never felt before.

I was about eight years old. There were five of us kids, all close in age, each one trying to help in whatever way we could. Our little house was always filled with noise and laughter, and even though it was cramped, it felt like home. But that year was a hard one. My daddy had taken ill during the late summer, and Mama was doing her best to keep things going. She took on sewing for neighbors and mended clothes when she could, but times were leaner than usual. We all tried to help; my older brother worked odd jobs on the weekends, and I remember walking up and down the road, looking for anything I could collect and sell—cans, bottles, or even just scrap wood.

As Christmas drew near, I could feel the air was different that year. Normally, there was a little excitement buzzing in our home, a feeling of anticipation even though we knew to keep our hopes low. But that year, there was a quietness in my parents' voices, a look in Mama's eyes that seemed sadder, more tired. She'd look at each of us as if she was trying to memorize our faces, as though she was holding on to something that didn't want to stay.

We didn't say much about Christmas that December. We knew the money wasn't there, even for the small things. But in my heart, I held out a little hope. I thought maybe, just maybe, my daddy would find a way to surprise us, to make something out of nothing like he always did. He'd taken to carving small wooden toys in the past years, whittling with his pocketknife by the fire, but that year, he barely had the energy to hold up his hand, let alone carve anything. I remember watching him, his rough hands weathered from years of work, now shaking, looking too frail to be the hands of the man I knew as my daddy.

Christmas morning came, and we all gathered around the little tree, knowing deep down what to expect. I looked at the tree—bare of ornaments except for a few pinecones we'd collected and a strip of fabric Mama had tied in a bow. Beneath it was empty, the floor as bare as I'd ever seen it on Christmas. I looked at my younger sister, who had her hands wrapped around her knees, her eyes filled with quiet wonder. She was too young to understand why there weren't any gifts, and she whispered to me, "Maybe they're hiding, like a surprise?" I wanted so badly to believe her, to tell her she was right. But I just put my arm around her and sat still, wishing for the words that wouldn't come.

Mama tried her best to cheer us up. She had baked a little bread and spread it with a dab of homemade jam she'd been saving. We each got a slice, and though I could see the sadness in her face, she tried to smile, to keep her voice steady as she said, "Christmas isn't just about what you get, it's about who you have." But I knew, even then, that her heart was breaking as much as ours. She wanted to give us the world, but life had been too hard that year.

As we sat together that morning, huddled close for warmth, my daddy cleared his throat, trying to gather his voice. He told us stories about his own Christmases growing up, how his father had made toys from bits of tin or scraps of wood, how they'd sung carols by the fire, and how his mama had made every Christmas feel like a blessing. He told us, "Sometimes, life doesn't give you the things you want, but it's in those times you find out what you're made of, what really matters."

I looked around at my brothers and sisters, each one of them quiet, each one holding back the same mix of disappointment and gratitude. There was no paper to tear, no toys to share, but in that moment, there was a kind of closeness, a kind of love that went beyond anything we could wrap or open.

That day, we played outside in the snow, throwing snowballs, building forts, and finding joy in each other. I think we were each trying to make the best of it, finding ways to laugh and forget the heaviness in our hearts. We found bits of broken tree branches and carved them into sticks, pretending they were swords, running around until our cheeks were pink and our hands numb from the cold.

Looking back, that Christmas without presents taught me more than any toy or gift ever could. It taught me the strength of family, the importance of being there for one another, and the value of love that goes beyond material things. My parents gave us the best gift they could that year, even if they didn't realize it. They showed us resilience, love, and sacrifice—themes that would carry us through the hardest times and keep us bound to each other in ways I could never explain.

Christmas is about so much more than what's under the tree—it's about who's around it. And even on that cold, empty morning in Appalachia, my family was there, our love shining as brightly as any Christmas star.

Christmas Church Services in Appalachia: A Walk Down Memory Lane

Growing up in Tazewell County, Virginia, Christmas was more than just a holiday; it was a season of tradition, a time when the chill in the air seemed to bring folks closer together. One of the most special parts of the season for me was going to church the week before Christmas. Our little church, nestled right off a winding mountain road, was a gathering place not just for Sunday services but for sharing in the warmth of community, especially during the Christmas season.

Our church wasn't anything fancy. It was a simple white clapboard building with a tall steeple and a bell that you could hear echoing down the valley each Sunday morning. Inside, the pews were worn and creaky, and the windows were the kind that frosted up as the cold of December settled in. But to us, it was the grandest place on earth. It was the heart of our community, a place filled with familiar faces, comforting hymns, and the spirit of something bigger than ourselves.

As Christmas drew closer, the church transformed into a winter wonderland in its own humble way. Folks from the congregation would gather on a Saturday before the big service, bundling up against the cold, bringing pine branches, candles, and red ribbons to decorate the altar and aisles. I remember the scent of pine filling the room, mingling with the faint lingering scent of wood smoke from the old stove in the corner that barely warmed the room but was all we had. Someone would bring in a small Christmas tree, hand-cut from one of the nearby hillsides, and the women would decorate it with handmade ornaments, old-fashioned paper stars, and ribbons, the same ones they'd use year after year.

On the Sunday before Christmas, everyone would dress in their best, ready to celebrate. Mama would make sure we were polished up, our clothes neat, and our shoes shined, even if they were a bit scuffed. My sisters wore little woolen hats and mittens, and I remember my daddy helping me button up my coat with a gentle hand on my shoulder. The chill outside made every breath a puff of white, but there was warmth in knowing we were about to spend time with friends, family, and neighbors.

Walking up to the church that morning was like stepping into a page of a Christmas story. The sun would just be rising over the hills, casting a pink and orange glow across the snow-dusted mountains. The quiet was profound, broken only by the crunch of our boots in the snow and the sound of voices as folks gathered on the front steps, greeting each other with hearty handshakes and warm smiles.

The service itself was always magical. Our preacher would stand at the pulpit, his voice a mix of reverence and joy as he read the story of Christ's birth, recounting it as if he was there himself. The older folks would nod along, lips moving in silent agreement, and the kids—though sometimes squirming in the pews—would listen, wide-eyed, as if hearing it for the first time. Our preacher spoke with such tenderness, as if he wanted each of us to feel the hope and promise in that story. He'd talk about how Mary and Joseph traveled those long, cold miles to Bethlehem, how there was no room for them at the inn, and how even in a humble stable, the world was given its greatest gift.

But my favorite part of the service was the singing. Oh, how we'd sing! "Silent Night," "O Holy Night," "Angels We Have Heard on High"—each song seemed to fill every corner of that little church. Mama would sing beside me, her voice soft and steady, and sometimes I'd see a tear in her eye, especially during "Silent Night." I didn't understand back then what moved her so deeply, but I could feel it in the way she held my hand, her fingers warm around mine as she sang.

There was a moment, always towards the end of the service, when the pastor would dim the lights, and each of us would hold a candle. One by one, he'd light the first candle and pass it down the row, each of us carefully tilting our own to catch the flame. Soon, the whole room would be aglow, each face illuminated by the soft, flickering light. We'd sing "Silent Night" together, and in that warm candlelight, it felt as though time had stopped. For that moment, the worries of the world—the hard winter, the tough times, the lean years—seemed to fade away. All that was left was peace, love, and the quiet knowledge that we were surrounded by people who truly cared.

After the service, we'd all gather outside, our breath making little clouds in the cold, laughing, hugging, and wishing each other Merry Christmas. Some of the women would hand out brown paper bags filled with treats—an apple, some hard candy, and maybe a handful of nuts. It wasn't much, but to us kids, it felt like a treasure. Those small gestures—the bags of treats, the shared songs, the gentle hugs—were like gifts in themselves, little reminders of how much we meant to each other.

Back then, we didn't have a lot, but those Christmas services filled us with something that went beyond gifts or money. They gave us a feeling of hope, a reminder that we were part of something bigger—a family, a community, a faith that bound us together through thick and thin. The lights, the gifts, the decorations—they're all wonderful, but nothing will ever compare to the feeling of those Christmas services in Appalachia, where our hearts were full, our voices joined, and our spirits lifted in the true meaning of Christmas.

My Mother's Christmas Tradition: Sausage Balls and Holiday Cheer

There's something magical about the holidays—a time when family comes together, the house glows with twinkling lights, and traditions bring a comforting sense of home. For me, one memory shines brighter than most: watching my mom make her famous sausage balls while we decorated for Christmas.

It always started early in the morning, when the air outside was crisp and the frost sparkled on the windows. Mom would pull out her tattered recipe card, the one with smudges and little notes in the margins, and start gathering her ingredients. The smell of sausage, sharp cheddar, and biscuit mix would soon fill the kitchen, wrapping the whole house in warmth.

With flour-dusted hands, she'd patiently roll each ball of dough, humming Christmas carols under her breath. I remember sneaking into the kitchen to "help," though I was really there to steal a pinch of cheese or a taste of the mix. She never minded—she just smiled and told me to grab a baking sheet.

Meanwhile, the living room came alive. My siblings and I would work on the tree, carefully placing ornaments that had been in the family for years. Some were handmade, others had stories behind them—a reindeer I painted in kindergarten, a fragile glass angel from Grandma. The lights would flicker on, and we'd stand back, debating whether we'd overdone it or if we needed more sparkle.

Mom would step in every so often, balancing her baking with helping us untangle a strand of lights or fix a crooked bow on a wreath. But when the sausage balls came out of the oven, everything stopped. The tray would land on the counter, and we'd all gather, plates in hand, to grab those warm, cheesy bites. They tasted like Christmas—savory, comforting, and made with love.

It wasn't just the sausage balls, though they were undeniably delicious. It was the way Mom made everything feel special— the music playing softly in the background, the glow of the fireplace, the laughter as we argued over who hung the best ornament. Even the slightly lopsided tree topper was perfect in its own way because it was ours.

Now, as an adult, I've carried on the tradition. Every Christmas, I find myself in the kitchen, rolling dough and humming carols, just like Mom did. And when I see my own kids decorating the tree, their faces lit with excitement, I feel that same magic she created for us.

Mom's sausage balls weren't just food—they were a piece of her, a little tradition that brought us all together. And now, they're a piece of me too, a reminder that the simplest things often make the holidays the most meaningful.

Stringing Popcorn on the Christmas Tree: Memories from a Mountain Christmas

Of all the Christmas traditions we shared, one of my favorites was stringing popcorn for the tree. It was such a small thing, yet it filled our home with joy, marking the official beginning of the holiday season.

We didn't have the glossy store-bought ornaments you see everywhere now. Money was tight, so we got creative with what we had. Mama believed that Christmas was meant to be celebrated with things made by hand and from the heart, so we'd make our decorations ourselves. There was a feeling of excitement as soon as December rolled in—my brothers, sisters, and I would watch as Mama pulled out her big sewing needle and an old spool of thread from her sewing box, knowing it was time to start stringing popcorn for the tree.

Now, popping the popcorn itself was an event. We didn't use a fancy popcorn maker; we had an old iron pot we'd set on the stove. I remember standing around, listening for those first pops as the kernels heated up, filling the air with that toasty, warm smell. When it was ready, Mama would pour it into a big bowl, and we'd try to pick out the fluffiest pieces, setting them aside for the stringing. We kids were supposed to be careful not to snack on it, but I think we ate just as much as we strung!

Once we had our popcorn ready, Mama would thread the needle and give each of us our own length of thread. We'd sit in a circle on the floor, watching the fire flicker in the fireplace, and start carefully pushing the needle through each piece. It was slow, careful work, especially since you had to go easy or the popcorn would just crumble in your hands. My little sister usually needed help, her fingers too small to manage the needle without getting poked. Mama would sit beside her, guiding her hands gently, showing her how to handle each kernel. It wasn't fancy, but it was beautiful, watching that simple white chain grow as we worked, laughing and chatting away.

Sometimes, we'd add in cranberries, bright red against the white of the popcorn. A neighbor would share a bag of them, or Daddy would trade for some at the general store, and we'd scatter them along the string to give it a touch of color. The bright red against the white made it look so festive, a bit like a garland of red berries sprinkled across the snow. Every once in a while, we'd make strings out of whatever we could find—some years it was just popcorn, other times we added dried orange slices or bits of colored paper we'd cut out and twisted along the string.

When the strings were ready, we'd all help put them on the tree. We didn't have a big, full tree like the ones you see in magazines. Ours was usually a little scraggly, cut down from the side of the mountain by Daddy and one of my older brothers. The branches were thin and uneven, but to us, it was perfect. We'd start at the top and drape the strings all the way down, filling in any empty spaces with care. There was something so magical about it, watching that little tree come to life with the decorations we'd made ourselves.

And that was our Christmas tree—no tinsel, no store-bought lights, just simple popcorn strings, maybe a few pinecones we'd collected and dusted with flour to look like snow, and some ribbons Mama had saved up. We'd turn off all the lights except for the fire, letting its soft glow light up the tree and cast shadows across the room. We'd sit back on the floor, admiring our work, proud of what we'd done together. Even though it was simple, it felt like the most beautiful tree in the world.

When Christmas morning finally came, we'd open our gifts— often handmade scarves, mittens, or maybe a toy carved by Daddy—and we'd sit by the tree, still draped in the popcorn strings we'd made with our own hands. That tree was more than just a decoration; it was a reminder of the love and time we shared as a family. Those strings of popcorn were more than just a garland—they were a thread that bound us together, each kernel, each string holding a memory we'd made as we laughed, talked, and created something beautiful in our own humble way.

The day after Christmas, Mama would carefully take down the popcorn strings and hang them outside for the birds and animals to enjoy. I'd watch as the sparrows, cardinals, and chickadees picked at the strings, a feast for them during the cold of winter. It was a little way of giving back, a reminder that even in the hardest months, we were part of something bigger. That simple string of popcorn, made with love, would help see other creatures through the long winter.

Christmas 1973: A Coal Strike Christmas in Harlan County, Kentucky

When I think back to the Christmas of 1973, it's hard not to feel a pang of heartache, but also a swell of pride. That was the year the Brookside coal strike hit us hardest. Daddy was out on strike with the union, standing shoulder to shoulder with other miners, demanding a fair contract from the company. It was a battle fought with grit and resolve, but it came at a cost—especially during the holidays.

We'd always been a family that didn't have much, but we made do. That year, though, even "making do" felt like a stretch. The strike had dragged on for months, and with no pay coming in, every dollar had to stretch further than it ever had before. Mom tried to shield us from the worst of it, but we weren't blind. We saw the empty spaces in the pantry, the worn soles on Daddy's work boots, and the worry that creased her forehead when she thought we weren't looking.

But if there's one thing about my family—and about Appalachians in general—it's that we don't quit, and we sure don't let hard times rob us of what matters most. Even with Daddy out on the picket line and the company playing hardball, Mom was determined we'd still have Christmas.

We started early, weeks before the big day, getting ready in ways that didn't cost a dime. Mom sent us out into the woods behind the house to gather pine branches, holly sprigs, and anything else that could make the house feel festive. My little brother Tommy found a scraggly cedar tree that wasn't much taller than he was, and we lugged it home, laughing the whole way because the trunk was so crooked it leaned like it was trying to run away.

Decorating that little tree became a family affair. We didn't have store-bought ornaments, but Mom had a way of making magic out of nothing. She handed us scraps of fabric to cut into stars and tied red ribbons from her sewing basket into bows. We strung popcorn and cranberries—well, mostly cranberries, since we couldn't afford to waste much popcorn—and draped the garlands around the tree. By the time we were done, that crooked cedar stood proud in the corner of our living room, glowing with the kind of beauty only love and effort can create.

Gifts were another matter entirely. Mom sat us down one night and gently explained that Santa might have a hard time making it to our house this year, what with so many kids to visit and Daddy being out of work. We nodded solemnly, pretending to understand, but deep down, we were worried that Christmas morning might feel empty.

But as Christmas Day approached, something remarkable happened. Neighbors started showing up at our door, each carrying a little something to share. Mrs. Hawkins brought over a pan of cornbread and a jar of apple butter. The Millers down the road dropped off a bag of walnuts and a small sack of oranges. And Mr. Turner, who had no family of his own, showed up with a sack of coal—"to keep your fire warm," he said, though his eyes told us he knew it was more than that.

The day before Christmas, Daddy came home from the picket line early, carrying a sack over his shoulder. We watched with wide eyes as he pulled out little gifts he'd managed to trade for—a used puzzle for me, a toy truck for Tommy, and a book of poems for Mom. He'd worked out the trades with other union families, all of them doing their best to give their kids something to smile about despite the strike.

On Christmas morning, we sat around that little tree, our bellies warm from the biscuits and gravy Mom had somehow managed to whip up. We opened our gifts one by one, each met with cheers and laughter. That puzzle may as well have been gold to me, and Eddie looked like the happiest boy in the world pushing his truck across the floor.

But the best part of that Christmas wasn't the gifts or even the food—it was the way our family and community came together. The strike might've kept paychecks out of our pockets, but it couldn't touch the strength of the people in Harlan County. We shared what we had, leaned on each other, and proved that the spirit of Christmas doesn't come from stores or money. It comes from love, resilience, and the belief that better days are worth fighting for.

Now, years later, I look back on that Christmas as one of the hardest, but also one of the most meaningful, I've ever known. It taught me that even in the toughest of times, there's always light to be found if you're willing to create it. Daddy eventually went back to work, and life got a little easier, but the lessons of that Christmas have stayed with me ever since. Sometimes, the hardest seasons teach you the most about what truly matters.

Christmas Visits with Family in Appalachia: Memories to Last a Lifetime

Christmas was always a season of togetherness, laughter, and simple joys. But there was one part of it that meant more than anything: going to visit family, especially my grandparents. As soon as Thanksgiving passed, the anticipation began to build. The days grew colder, the nights longer, and our hearts warmer with the thought of piling into the old family car to make the journey to see the people we loved most.

The drive to my grandparents' house was always an adventure in itself. We didn't live far, but the winding mountain roads made it feel like we were traveling to some distant, magical place. The car would be packed with blankets, a thermos of hot chocolate, and a tin of Mama's freshly baked gingerbread. My siblings and I would be bundled up in our winter coats, noses pressed against the frosted windows, watching as the world slipped by in a blur of bare trees and snow-dusted hills. The mountains seemed to stretch out forever, rising up to meet the sky, like silent guardians keeping watch over us. There was a certain comfort in those mountains, a feeling that no matter how cold or hard life might get, they would always stand steady and strong.

When we'd finally pull up to my grandparents' old house, my heart would race with excitement. Their home was nestled in a little valley, surrounded by tall, snow-covered pines that looked like they belonged in a Christmas card. I can still remember the way the windows glowed with warm yellow light, the faint smell of wood smoke coming from the chimney, and the sight of my grandmother standing at the door, wiping her hands on her apron, a big smile spreading across her face as she opened her arms to greet us.

There was nothing quite like stepping into my grandparents' house at Christmastime. The air was thick with the smell of pine, cinnamon, and whatever delicious dish Grandma had cooking in the oven. Her kitchen was always filled with warmth, laughter, and enough food to feed an army. There'd be jars of preserves on the counter, stacks of homemade biscuits, and a big pot of soup simmering on the stove. And there was always a plate of molasses cookies waiting for us kids—soft, sticky, and sweet as could be. Grandpa would be in his chair by the fire, his old pipe in hand, smiling as we tumbled through the door, our voices filling the quiet room.

Christmas at my grandparents' was filled with little traditions, ones that seemed simple but have stayed with me my whole life. In the evenings, we'd all gather in the living room around the tree. Their Christmas tree wasn't fancy—just a small, scrappy pine that Grandpa would cut down himself from the edge of their property—but to us, it was the most beautiful tree in the world. It would be decorated with handmade ornaments, strings of popcorn, and a few treasured glass baubles that had been passed down for generations. Grandma would pull out a box of decorations, each one a little memory from Christmases past, and we'd hang them with care, listening to her stories about where each one came from.

One of my favorite traditions was when Grandpa would sit us kids down and tell us stories from his own childhood Christmases. He'd talk about how they made do with so little back then, about getting an orange or a single piece of candy as a gift, and how even that felt like the biggest treat in the world. I'd listen, eyes wide, trying to imagine a time when life was even harder than it was for us. But there was never a hint of sadness in his voice, just gratitude and joy for the simple things, for family, and for the memories that stayed with him through the years.

Christmas Eve was always a magical night. We'd all gather around the fire, wrapped in blankets, sipping hot cider as Grandpa read the story of Jesus' birth from an old, worn Bible. His voice was gentle and steady, filling the room with a sense of peace and reverence. Even as kids, we could feel the importance of the moment, the way his words brought the story to life, connecting us to something bigger than ourselves. And when he finished, we'd sit in silence for a moment, just listening to the crackle of the fire, each of us lost in our own thoughts.

Later, we'd all bundle up and step outside to look up at the stars. The mountain air was so cold it felt like it would freeze your breath, but the sky was crystal clear, a blanket of stars stretching out above us, so close it felt like you could reach out and touch them. Grandpa would point out the constellations, his finger tracing patterns in the sky, and I'd feel a shiver of wonder at the beauty of it all, the feeling that in that quiet moment, we were a part of something timeless.

On Christmas morning, we'd wake up early, excited to see what little gifts might be waiting for us. We didn't expect much—usually just a few small presents, maybe a book, a warm scarf Grandma had knitted, or a handful of candy. But it wasn't about the gifts themselves; it was about the laughter, the hugs, and the joy of being together. My grandparents would sit back, smiling as we tore through the wrapping, their eyes filled with the kind of love that can't be put into words.

After breakfast, we'd all head outside for a walk through the snowy woods, our boots crunching in the snow, our breaths visible in the crisp morning air. The mountains were so quiet, so peaceful, like they were holding their breath in reverence for the day. We'd explore the trails, laughing and calling to each other, the sound echoing off the hills, a reminder that in that moment, we were exactly where we belonged.

As the day wore on, more family would arrive—uncles, aunts, cousins—all piling into that little house until it was bursting at the seams. There'd be more food, more stories, and more laughter, filling the rooms with a warmth that went beyond the fire in the hearth. Those were the moments that made Christmas so special, the feeling that we were all connected, part of something much bigger than ourselves.

Christmas in Appalachia wasn't about gifts or decorations. It was about family, tradition, and the love that held us all together, year after year. And even though those days are long gone, their memory lives on, a little piece of home I carry with me always.

A Strange and Special Christmas Tradition

Growing up in the heart of Appalachia, Christmas wasn't just a season—it was an experience unlike anything else. We didn't have grand stores or elaborate parades, but what we lacked in extravagance, we more than made up for in unique traditions. Of all the quirky, heartfelt rituals my family practiced, one stands out as both strange and unforgettable: our "Christmas Possum Parade."

Now, I know what you're thinking—what could possibly be festive about a possum? Let me explain. It all started with my great-grandpa, a true Appalachian character if there ever was one. He was a storyteller, a hunter, and a man with a sharp wit who loved turning simple things into cherished memories. One Christmas Eve, back in the 1940s, he spotted a possum nosing around the woodpile behind the house. Rather than chase it off, he decided to "welcome" it into the holiday festivities.

He grabbed his fiddle, called the kids outside, and started playing a lively tune as he followed the possum around the yard. The family joined in, clapping, laughing, and stomping their feet in time with the music. That scruffy possum scurried off eventually, but the impromptu celebration stuck. Every year after that, Grandpa would bring out his fiddle on Christmas Eve, and the "possum parade" became a family tradition.

By the time I was born, the tradition had evolved into something even wilder. We didn't wait for a real possum to show up anymore—that was too unreliable. Instead, my uncle crafted a "parade possum" out of papier-mâché and an old mop handle. It was a masterpiece of Appalachian ingenuity: a painted gray body with googly eyes, a coiled wire tail, and a little Santa hat perched jauntily on its head.

On Christmas Eve, as soon as darkness fell, we'd bundle up in our coats and scarves and gather outside. The oldest family member (usually Grandpa, until he passed the torch to my dad) would lead the parade with the possum on a stick, twirling it like a majorette leading a band. Behind him came the rest of us, stomping, clapping, and singing carols at the top of our lungs. Someone always brought a fiddle, and another cousin might beat on an old washtub or clang spoons together for rhythm.

We'd snake our way through the yard, down the dirt road, and sometimes even to the neighbors' houses, hollering "Merry Christmas!" like a ragtag Appalachian caroling troupe. Every so often, someone would let out a mock "possum call," a high-pitched yowl that never failed to make the younger kids collapse in giggles.

The grand finale of the parade was the "Possum Toss." We'd gather around the bonfire Grandpa always built for the occasion, and the leader would ceremonially "toss" the papier-mâché possum into the air. Of course, no one actually let it hit the flames—we were too attached to that goofy creation. Someone would catch it, and we'd all cheer like we'd just won the biggest Christmas game ever played.

Looking back, I realize how absurd the whole thing must sound. But to us, it was magical. It wasn't about the possum itself—it was about the laughter, the music, and the sheer joy of being together. In those moments, we weren't just celebrating Christmas; we were celebrating family, creativity, and the Appalachian spirit of making the most out of whatever you have.

It might not be the kind of tradition you'd read about in a glossy holiday magazine, but it's ours. And for me, it's a reminder that the strangest traditions are often the most meaningful—the ones that make your family uniquely yours.

Remembering Mama's Christmas Spirit in the Appalachian Mountains

When I think back on my childhood growing up in East Tennessee, no memory shines brighter than my mother's love for Christmas. She brought magic to our home every December, filling it with warmth, laughter, and the unmistakable smell of baking bread. Mama didn't need glittering lights or expensive gifts to make Christmas special. Her love, her creativity, and her belief in the magic of the season were all we needed.

Our house was small, at the head of the holler, with the mountain rising up behind us like a protective giant. Winters were cold, and the wind would howl through the gaps in the windows, but as soon as Mama started her Christmas preparations, that chill seemed to be replaced with a sense of coziness and joy. I remember coming home from school one crisp afternoon, stomping the snow off my boots and shaking the cold from my coat, only to walk into a house transformed.

Mama would be hanging up handmade paper snowflakes, and every surface would be adorned with a bit of greenery she'd cut from the pine trees out back.

Decorating the tree was a family affair, though Mama was always the driving force. We didn't have fancy ornaments or tinsel. Instead, she'd pull out a box filled with decorations we'd made ourselves over the years—strings of popcorn, paper stars, and pinecones we'd gathered from the woods and dusted with flour to look like snow. Every year, she would unwrap a set of small knitted ornaments that she had made as a young girl, and she'd tell us about how her mother taught her to knit in front of the fireplace one snowy winter. These simple ornaments felt magical to me because they held stories, passed down through Mama's loving hands.

And then there was her baking. Mama didn't bake much during the year, but come December, she would spend hours in our tiny kitchen, turning out pies, cookies, and breads that filled the air with warmth and sweetness. Her molasses cookies were my favorite, spicy and soft, and she'd cut them into little tree shapes, dusting them with sugar. On some days, she'd let me help, her hands guiding mine as I pressed the cutter into the dough, her laughter ringing out as I tried to sneak a taste. Those cookies tasted like Christmas to me, like love and magic all wrapped up in one.

Mama also had a heart for helping others, and she believed that Christmas was a time to be kind and give back, no matter how little we had. Each year, she would pull out her sewing kit and spend hours mending blankets and stitching up little gifts to give to neighbors who might be struggling. I remember how she'd quietly slip a bag of cookies or a jar of her homemade preserves into a basket, leaving them on someone's porch with a little note. She never expected anything in return; her joy came from knowing that she was spreading love, even if only in a small way.

One of the best parts of the holiday season was Christmas Eve, when the house would be filled with the scent of pine and the soft glow of candlelight. Mama would sit us down in the living room, wrapped in blankets, and read the Christmas story from an old, worn Bible. Her voice was gentle and soothing, and I'd watch the way her eyes softened with love as she spoke. She would tell us that Christmas wasn't about what we had or didn't have; it was about the love we shared and the blessings that came from being together. I don't know if I fully understood her words then, but I remember the way they made me feel: safe, warm, and deeply loved.

Christmas morning was never filled with mountains of gifts, but somehow Mama made it feel like the most magical day of the year. We'd each receive a few small, thoughtful gifts—maybe a hand-sewn doll, a book she had managed to save up for, or a new pair of mittens. She'd wrap each present carefully, using whatever paper or ribbons she could find, and watching us open them filled her with a joy that I can still see in my mind. Mama taught us that Christmas wasn't about the things we received; it was about the love we shared as a family.

Now that I'm older, I see all the ways Mama's Christmas spirit lives on in me. When December rolls around, I find myself doing the same things she did—baking cookies, decorating with simple things from the woods, giving quietly where I can. Most importantly, I always remember to take time to honor the birth of our savior, Jesus. I look back and realize that Mama didn't just love Christmas; she was Christmas to us. She embodied everything that made the season special: love, generosity, kindness, and a belief in the beauty of small, simple things.

I'll never forget those Christmases in our little house in the holler. They were a reminder that even with so little, we had everything, because we had her. Mama's love, her laughter, and her faith in the spirit of Christmas filled our hearts and warmed our home in a way that no amount of gifts or glittering lights ever could. And though she's gone now, her memory fills my heart every Christmas, reminding me of the beauty of love, family, and the magic that only a mother's heart can bring.

Operation Christmas Tree: A Tale of Too Big, Too Funny

Christmas was a special time filled with love, family, and more than a few comical mishaps. One year stands out particularly, when a family "operation" to get the perfect Christmas tree went hilariously sideways.

It was the week before Christmas, and Mama decided our usual Charlie Brown tree wasn't going to cut it that year. So, she sent Daddy and my older brother Billy out to find the "biggest, fullest, most beautiful tree the mountain has to offer." They headed off with an old axe, a rope, and the family truck, and Mama watched them go with a look of excitement in her eye, rubbing her hands together like this was going to be our best Christmas yet.

Hours later, we heard the rumble of the truck coming down the road. Mama, my little sister, and I ran outside, and there it was—a tree so big it was practically dragging behind the truck. I could see Daddy's satisfied grin from twenty feet away. It was a monster of a tree, and I had no idea how they thought it was going to fit in our little living room. This tree was so huge that it would have made Clark Griswold blush.

The whole family pitched in, hauling it inside through the narrow doorway, needles flying everywhere, my siblings giggling the entire time. Daddy was trying to wrangle it through the front door when we heard a SNAP followed by a WHOOSH, and half the tree's branches went tumbling off, scattering pine needles like confetti.

Mama shook her head, "That's what you get for bringing a whole forest inside!"

Undeterred, Daddy propped it up in the corner and declared it "perfectly rustic." We spent the next few hours decorating it as best as we could, trying to hide the bald spots with tinsel and popcorn strings. Every time someone brushed past it, more needles rained down. Mama finally had to sweep them up in a big pile, saying we'd have enough for a second Christmas tree at this rate!

But the real hilarity came later that night. Daddy had found some old electric lights and strung them up around the tree, but the wiring must have been as old as he was. We were sitting by the fire, admiring our "masterpiece," when suddenly there was a loud POP! The lights blinked off, and the entire room went dark. After a moment of stunned silence, Daddy sighed, "Guess that tree was too big for its own good."

Mama started laughing so hard she had tears in her eyes, and pretty soon we were all laughing, too. Even Daddy, who rarely cracked a smile, shook his head with a grin. For the rest of that Christmas, we had a half-bare, half-sparkly tree, sitting proudly in the corner, and it's still one of my favorite memories.

That year we learned that "bigger isn't always better" when it comes to Christmas trees. Mama told us it would be a Christmas we'd never forget—and she was right.

The Magic of the Santa Train: A Marrowbone Christmas Tradition

Growing up in Marrowbone, Kentucky, nothing was more exciting than the arrival of the Santa Train. Every November, just as the air got that first real bite of winter chill, the whole town would buzz with excitement about that train's yearly trip through the Appalachians. The Santa Train, loaded up with gifts, toys, clothes, and candy, made its way from Shelbiana, Kentucky, all the way to Kingsport, Tennessee, winding its way through the mountains and stopping at small towns along the route. And we'd wait eagerly for that one special day when it would pull through our little town.

As a kid, I'd count down the days until the Santa Train arrived. My friends and I would talk about it at school, trying to guess what kind of treasures might be on board this year. Some years, a few of the boys swore they'd seen Santa himself on the train, throwing out toys like he was tossing candy. That image filled my young mind with wonder, and I'd dream about seeing Santa waving from the train car, his red suit bright against the winter landscape.

The morning the train was scheduled to come through, I'd be up early, bundled in my warmest clothes. Mama would wrap me up in a too-big scarf, tug a hat over my ears, and pack us all up with hot chocolate in an old thermos. My siblings and I would join the crowd, shuffling down the dirt road toward the tracks, eyes peeled for the first sign of that distant whistle.

We'd gather on the hill near the tracks with nearly everyone in Marrowbone. The air would be thick with the sound of voices and laughter, a mix of kids fidgeting with excitement and parents holding cups of steaming coffee. Finally, we'd hear it—the faint, magical sound of the train whistle echoing through the valley, growing louder as the Santa Train chugged around the bend.

The train itself was a sight to see. As it got closer, the crowd would start cheering, and kids would jump up and down, holding onto their parents' hands. Some of the men would wave their hats, and the women would wave their hands in the air, all eyes locked on the bright train rolling toward us. With red and green decorations wrapped around the railcars and volunteers tossing candy out to the crowd, it was like something out of a Christmas story.

When the train finally came to a stop, cheers would fill the air. The Santa Train volunteers, bundled up in coats, would begin passing out bags of candy and small presents—little toys, stuffed animals, and sometimes even clothes. We'd reach up, wide-eyed, trying to catch a bag or two. For some families in our town, those small gifts were the highlight of Christmas. They meant a lot to all of us, not because they were fancy or expensive, but because they felt like a special piece of magic coming right down the tracks just for us.

And then, the best part of all—Santa himself would appear. With a hearty "Ho, ho, ho!" he'd wave from the railcar, calling out to the children. I remember the first time I saw him, his red suit standing out so bright against the snowy hills. He'd call out, telling us to be good, to listen to our parents, and to take care of one another. It felt like he was talking directly to me, and my heart would swell with pure wonder.

There was something so special, so uplifting, about watching the Santa Train come through town. It felt like a reminder that even tucked away in our small, quiet town in the Appalachian Mountains, we were part of something bigger, something magical and full of kindness. That train carried more than toys and treats; it carried the spirit of Christmas and the warmth of community.

After the train pulled away and the last whistles faded into the distance, we'd all walk back home, huddled together, chatting excitedly about what we'd gotten and what we'd seen. For the rest of the season, those little treasures from the Santa Train would remind us of that magical morning and the special visit from Santa.

The Christmas Orange: A Simple Gift of Sunshine

Christmastime was full of simple joys and traditions that meant the world to us, and nothing symbolized that better than the bright, cheerful orange we'd each get in our stockings. For kids today, it might be hard to imagine just how special that orange was, but back then, it was one of the greatest Christmas treats we could dream of.

Back in those days, fresh fruit was a rarity in our mountain town, especially in the winter. Apples from the fall harvest would last us a little while, but an orange—that was pure magic. Those oranges didn't come easy either. Daddy would often have to save up or make a trip down to the general store just to get a few for Christmas. It was a luxury, and we all knew it, which made it feel even more precious.

Christmas morning, we'd rush out of bed, excited to see what small gifts and treats might be waiting for us. We didn't have fancy stockings; Mama would hang up a pair of our cleanest socks, stretched to the brim with a few goodies. And sure enough, nestled down in the bottom of each one was a single, round, sun-colored orange. Just seeing that flash of bright color against the drab winter was like a gift in itself.

I remember holding that orange in my hands, the cool, bumpy skin smooth under my fingers. I'd lift it to my nose, breathing in that fresh, citrusy smell that was unlike anything else in our home. That smell was the scent of Christmas to us—the promise of a rare and treasured taste that only came around once a year.

Peeling it was a ritual all its own. Mama taught us to be careful, to savor the process. She'd help my little sister, Bertha, peel hers, taking the skin off in one long spiral if she could, as we all watched, captivated. The bright orange flesh glistened in the dim morning light, each segment like a little jewel. Sometimes we'd stretch it out, eating one piece at a time, savoring the burst of sweet, tart juice. Other times, I couldn't help myself and would eat the whole thing in a few bites, juice dribbling down my chin, feeling like I was tasting pure sunshine in the middle of winter.

Those oranges weren't just a treat—they were a symbol of love and care, something Mama and Daddy went out of their way to get, just to make Christmas that much more special. They couldn't give us fancy toys or lots of presents, but that orange reminded us how much they wanted to bring us joy. It was their way of making the season feel magical, even when times were lean.

A Christmas in the Coal Camps

Christmas in the coal camps of Appalachia was a time of simple joys and a whole lot of community spirit. Life was tough in those coal camps in McDowell County, West Virginia, with long hours and dangerous work. But come Christmas, even the hardest-working folks found time to celebrate, sharing what little they had to make the holiday feel special for everyone.

In the weeks leading up to Christmas, a sense of anticipation would build in the camp. Families didn't have much to spare, but they found creative ways to bring some holiday magic to those tiny homes. Men would go out to the nearby woods to cut down the best tree they could find—often scraggly by today's standards, but perfect to us. Back home, we'd decorate those trees with whatever we had: strings of popcorn, paper chains made from scraps of old newspaper, and bits of tin foil saved from other seasons. Mama would sometimes cut out stars from cardboard and dust them with a little flour to make them shine, and those simple decorations made our home feel just a little brighter.

The mining companies sometimes set up community Christmas events, too, knowing how much the families needed a break from the grind of daily life. Some years, they'd bring in Santa Claus, who'd come down to the camp to give out small gifts—candy, apples, maybe a small toy or two. Those gifts were a big deal to us kids, who didn't get much new throughout the year. I remember the awe of seeing Santa step down from a wagon or out of the back of a truck, his red suit a sharp contrast to the gray coal dust that blanketed most everything around us.

Churches played a big part in Christmas, too. The camp's little church would be decorated with what folks could gather—pine branches, holly, and maybe even some red berries found by the more daring kids who ventured into the woods. On Christmas Eve, the entire community would gather for a candlelight service, filling that small, drafty building with warmth and song. Those hymns echoing off the walls would bring us all together, our voices blending in harmony, our hearts filled with gratitude. For many families, that church service was the heart of Christmas, a moment to pause and give thanks for what they had.

On Christmas morning, we'd wake to whatever small surprises our parents had managed to gather. In our stockings—often just a pair of Daddy's old work socks—we might find an orange, a peppermint stick, or maybe a little toy. Sometimes, if the family had saved enough, there might be a real treat like a handful of nuts or hard candy. Those little gifts, simple as they were, felt like treasures because we knew how hard our parents worked to provide them.

And then, of course, there was the Christmas meal. Families pooled what they had, trading sugar for flour or a dozen eggs for a few strips of bacon to make a feast. The women would gather in one house or another, cooking up dishes that, while humble, were made with love and care. There'd be cornbread, maybe some ham if someone had butchered a hog that fall, and pies made from whatever fruit had been canned in the summer. For one day, we set aside the struggles and came together as one big, extended family. Kids played together, men told stories, and the women laughed and sang as they worked.

It wasn't a Christmas filled with glittering gifts or elaborate meals, but it was a celebration of community and connection. It reminded us that, even in the midst of hard times, we had each other, and that meant more than anything money could buy. We didn't need much to make Christmas special; just a warm fire, a few simple decorations, and the people we loved around us.

A Puppy for Christmas

The Christmas I got a puppy was one I'll never forget, and even now, the memory fills me with a warmth that can only come from childhood. I grew up in a small house nestled in the Appalachian hills of Grundy, Virginia, where winters were crisp, the snow piled high, and our lives were full of the quiet beauty of the mountains. Times were tough, and while we never went hungry, Mama and Daddy worked hard to make ends meet, so Christmas was always simple. But the year I turned eight, my Christmas wish was a big one: I wanted a dog more than anything in the world.

I'd been dreaming of a puppy for as long as I could remember. I'd see stray dogs here and there along the dirt roads, and I'd stop to pet them, wondering what it would be like to have a dog of my own, one that would follow me everywhere, sleep at the foot of my bed, and be my best friend. I knew, though, that a puppy was a big ask. But still, that year, when Mama asked what I wanted for Christmas, I couldn't help myself. "A puppy," I whispered. Her eyes softened, and she gave me a little smile, but I knew it was a long shot.

As December went on, I forgot about my wish for a puppy, caught up in all the other wonderful things about the season. There were decorations to make, strings of popcorn to thread for the tree, and cookies to bake with Mama. On Christmas Eve, we went to our tiny church for the candlelight service, where we sang carols and listened to the story of the Nativity. Snow was falling thick and heavy as we made our way home, the world hushed in that special way only a snow-covered night can be.

When we got home, Mama sent me off to bed early, which wasn't unusual. The sooner I was asleep, the sooner Christmas would come, she'd say. I lay there, the quiet excitement bubbling inside me, and finally drifted off, imagining the stockings and small presents I'd find in the morning.

I must have been deep asleep when I felt something warm and furry nuzzle against my cheek. I opened my eyes, blinking in the dim light, and there, staring back at me with big brown eyes, was the tiniest, most precious little puppy I'd ever seen. She had soft, tan fur with little white spots on her chest and paws, and she was looking at me with that kind of trust that only puppies have.

I sat up, completely stunned, feeling like I was in a dream. I gently lifted her, and she squirmed in my arms, giving me a little lick on the chin. I looked over and saw Mama and Daddy standing in the doorway, watching me with warm smiles. "Merry Christmas, sweetheart," Daddy whispered.

"Mama, Daddy... how did you...?" I stammered, completely unable to believe it.

Daddy knelt down beside me, petting the puppy's soft little head. "Well, your Mama and I had a feeling this little one belonged right here with you," he said, his voice gentle.

It turns out, they'd been planning it for months. A neighbor down the road had a dog that'd just had puppies, and they'd saved one for me, knowing how much I'd wanted a dog. Mama had even been knitting a little blanket, the same one that now lay in the box they'd placed by my bed.

I hugged the puppy close, feeling her tiny heartbeat against my chest. I named her Daisy, because she seemed as gentle and sweet as the little flowers I loved picking in the spring. From that moment on, Daisy was my shadow. She followed me everywhere—out to the fields, down the road to visit our neighbors, and even to the little creek where I'd sit and dream about all kinds of things.

As winter turned to spring, Daisy grew fast, her legs getting long and lanky, her paws always a bit too big for her. She was my constant companion, a loyal friend who listened to all my secrets and gave me comfort in the way only a dog can. I took care of her as best I could, making sure she was warm, fed, and loved. And she returned that love a thousandfold, always greeting me with a wagging tail and those big, trusting eyes.

Looking back, I realize that Christmas wasn't just about getting a puppy. It was about the love and sacrifice my parents put into making my dream come true. They went out of their way, saved what little they could, and made arrangements all so that I'd have a friend to grow up with.

Daisy stayed by my side for years, becoming a part of our family and my childhood. She grew old alongside me, a loyal friend until the very end. And every Christmas, I still think back to that snowy Christmas morning, that little tan and white puppy with eyes so big and brown, and my parents' quiet smiles as they watched me unwrap the greatest gift I could ever imagine. It was a gift of joy, love, and the kind of memories that stay with you forever.

The Scarf That Stole Christmas

One Christmas, back when I was about nine or ten, we all gathered around our little tree, with the wood stove crackling and everyone in a good holiday mood. The tree was covered in popcorn strings and a handful of ornaments we'd collected over the years, and underneath were a few carefully wrapped presents. We didn't have a whole pile of gifts, so each one was a bit of a mystery, and the excitement was high.

Now, Mama had her hands full every Christmas keeping the family organized, so each of us got one or two gifts, carefully labeled with hand-written tags. Somehow, though, in all the holiday hustle, a couple of those tags must've gotten mixed up.

When it was finally my turn, I eagerly picked up a rectangular box wrapped in paper with snowmen on it. The tag said "To: Ray," so I was sure this was the one I'd been eyeing all week— the one I just *knew* was the little pocketknife I'd asked for. I tore off the paper with all the enthusiasm of a kid who'd just struck gold, my mouth already forming the words to thank my parents for my future "hunting knife."

But when I opened the box, I didn't see anything remotely sharp or outdoorsy. Instead, there was a frilly, bright pink scarf with glittery little tassels on the end. It looked like something a grandmother would wear on a church Sunday, not something a kid would need for catching frogs and running around the mountains. I stared down at it, mouth open, completely confused. My brothers and sisters were staring too, a mix of confusion and barely held-back laughter on their faces.

My sister, bless her, let out a snort she couldn't hold back. She leaned over, peering at my face and then at the scarf, and said, "Well, don't you look *precious*, darlin'."

At this, the room burst into laughter, including Mama, who covered her mouth with her hand as she realized the mix-up. She came over and said, "Oh my stars, honey, that one was supposed to be for your Aunt Clara! She's been after a scarf all winter!"

But the damage was done, and my siblings wouldn't let it go. My brother piped up, "Why don't you model it for us, big guy?" and everyone burst out laughing again.

Not one to back down, I stood up, looped the scarf around my neck with a dramatic flair, and gave my best runway strut around the room, while my family doubled over laughing. Even Daddy, who rarely cracked a smile, was wiping tears from his eyes. "Well, son," he said between laughs, "you sure know how to make a scarf work."

The best part was that every Christmas afterward, Mama would wrap something funny up for me—sometimes it was a pair of old Aunt Clara's frilly gloves, another time it was one of her hats. And every time I'd play it up, posing like a model to the delight of my family. That mix-up became a tradition, something we all laughed about for years.

Looking back, I don't remember much about the presents I got as a kid, but that wrong gift—the glittery scarf and all the laughs it brought—turned out to be one of the best "presents" of them all.

Christmas Up North: A Journey Back to Simplicity

When I was a kid growing up in the mountains, Christmas was the time of year we'd gather close with family, the kind of simple holiday where the smell of wood smoke filled the air and Mama made enough biscuits and ham to feed a small army. But one year, Daddy announced we'd be spending Christmas with some relatives up North. I don't think any of us knew what to expect. To be honest, we'd barely been outside our own county, let alone all the way up to Cleveland, where my aunt and her family had moved years earlier.

The trip itself was a shock to my little country heart. We loaded up our old truck and drove miles and miles through mountains and snowy highways until the hills disappeared and were replaced by flat, endless roads. When we got to the city, I felt like I'd stepped onto a different planet. Skyscrapers loomed high above us, stretching up farther than any mountain I'd ever seen. The streets were packed with cars, lights flashing from every direction, people bustling around with barely a second glance at one another. I couldn't help but stare, wide-eyed, feeling like a small fish in an awfully big pond.

My aunt's house was in a bustling neighborhood with tall, narrow houses stacked up close together. It wasn't like the old farmhouse we had back home, surrounded by woods and fields where you could see stars as bright as lanterns in the night sky. Here, the air was thick with smoke from factories, and all I could smell was the metallic tinge of the city. But what caught me most was how folks up North celebrated Christmas.

They had a Christmas tree, just like we did, but theirs was as tall as the room would allow, strung with lights that blinked in patterns and ornaments that looked like they'd cost a small fortune. It wasn't like our scrappy little tree, decorated with strings of popcorn and handmade ornaments, each one with a story or memory behind it. There was something grand about their tree, almost intimidating, and it made me feel a little out of place.

The city Christmas lights were a whole different experience. We went downtown to see the holiday displays, and my jaw about dropped at the rows of giant Christmas figures, Santas, elves, and even a nativity scene that stretched across half a block. Folks bustled around with bags in their hands, dressed in fancy coats and hats that looked like they were meant more for show than warmth. I remember Mama pulling my coat a little tighter around me, probably sensing how out of sorts I felt.

When Christmas Eve rolled around, my aunt announced we'd all be heading to a midnight church service. Now, I'd been to plenty of Christmas Eve services back home in our tiny wooden church, where we'd bundle up and trudge through the snow, huddling together as the pastor read the Christmas story. But this was something else entirely. The church we went to was huge, bigger than anything I'd ever seen. It was filled with people, all dressed to the nines, and there was an organ that roared so loud it practically shook the walls.

They lit candles, just like we did back home, but it felt different in that big, bustling church. I missed the quiet warmth of our little congregation, where every face was familiar, and everyone sang off-key but with so much heart. Here, the choir was flawless, the music grand, but something was missing. I felt a little homesick for our own humble carol-singing, where even the cows out in the barn could hear us.

But the biggest shock came on Christmas morning when we gathered around for presents. There were boxes piled up, more than I'd ever seen under a tree, wrapped in shiny paper and big bows. I was given a few gifts myself—things like a toy I'd never heard of, a fancy scarf that was scratchy but "in style," and a book I'd probably need a dictionary to get through. My cousins got new clothes, electronics, and toys that lit up and made noise. They tore through the wrapping paper without so much as a second glance, moving on to the next box before the last was even open.

Back home, presents were simpler, and each one was treasured, handled carefully to make it last. I remember thinking of the Christmas I'd been given a single wooden sled Daddy had made himself, and the pride I felt pulling it up the hill all day with my brother. Here, the gifts were flashier, shinier, but I missed that simple joy, the feeling of receiving something made with love.

After dinner, when everyone else was dozing by the fire, I sat with Mama, looking out the window at the snow-covered city. I could see her face, and she looked a little sad, a little homesick too. We talked about how Christmas back home felt different— simpler, maybe, but somehow warmer. She wrapped her arm around me and whispered, "Christmas isn't in the fancy lights or the shiny presents. It's right here," and she tapped my chest, right over my heart.

When we finally packed up to head back home, I felt a weight lift off my shoulders. The mountains welcomed us back like old friends, the familiar curves of the hills and the smell of wood smoke drifting from chimneys as we drove through small towns.

That Christmas up North gave me a gift I hadn't expected—a new appreciation for what we had. I realized then how lucky I was to grow up in the mountains, surrounded by family who cherished the simple things. Back home, Christmas wasn't about the show or the fuss. It was about gathering close, making do with what we had, and sharing love in the quiet, comforting way that felt just right.

The Red Wagon of Christmas Past

Christmas was a time of pure wonder, wrapped in the simplest things. I remember waking up on a crisp December morning, the world outside still and quiet, with a layer of frost glistening on the trees. Inside, the smell of pine filled our little home, and there, under the tree, I found it—my first real Christmas gift, a small but well-loved red Radio Flyer wagon.

Money was always tight in our home, but my parents had somehow saved up enough for this little wagon, and it became my world. I hauled that wagon everywhere, filling it with firewood from the backyard, rocks and sticks from the creek, even stray kittens I found hiding in the barn. Each winter, I'd bundle up, pulling my wagon through snowdrifts, pretending it was a sled or a mighty chariot. In the summer, it transformed into a "delivery truck," bringing supplies to my forts scattered across the hills. That little wagon wasn't just a toy—it was a ticket to every adventure my young heart could dream up. Every scratch and ding on it told a story, a memory of laughter and exploration in those Appalachian hills. The wagon has long since rusted away, but the memories of that Christmas gift are as vivid as ever.

A Christmas in the Heart of the Hills

Christmas church services were at the heart of the season, bringing our whole community together in a way that felt special, sacred, and uniquely ours. The journey would start on a cold, quiet evening, bundling up in our Sunday best with scarves, coats, and gloves, and making our way down the winding roads to our little white church, set against the backdrop of the Appalachian mountains of Logan, West Virginia. Snow, if we were lucky, would dust the ground, and the stars seemed to shine a little brighter, as if lighting our path.

The church was simple but beautiful, decorated with fresh pine branches, red ribbons, and candles in the windows. The scent of cedar and pine, mixed with the warmth of old wooden pews, filled the space. There was something almost magical about gathering together in that small, close-knit building, warmed not just by a furnace but by the smiles and greetings of neighbors, friends, and family who'd all come to celebrate the season.

Our Christmas service was always filled with carols we knew by heart. When we all joined in singing, it felt like the voices of our community lifted up through the rafters and into the hills around us and on up to Heaven. The children's choir would often sing, their little voices ringing out with joy, and we'd all laugh at the inevitable out-of-tune note or shy glance to the crowd.

There was always a nativity play, too. It was a tradition for the children to dress up as shepherds, angels, and wise men. Baby Jesus was often played by the newest addition to the congregation, bundled up snug in a makeshift manger that had held countless babies before. The simplicity of it all—the costumes made from bathrobes and tinsel halos—made it all the more special. There were no flashy lights or grand stages, just the pure joy of retelling the story of that holy night.

After the service, everyone would gather outside, greeting each other and sharing Christmas wishes. Some years, if the snow was fresh, we'd linger for a bit, laughing as we made footprints in the snow or tossed a few snowballs. There was a warmth in the air that had nothing to do with the temperature. As we headed home, with hearts full and voices hoarse from singing, it felt like we were carrying the spirit of Christmas with us, ready to cherish it until the next year.

The memories of those candle-lit pews, familiar hymns, and the faces of everyone I loved remind me of the true spirit of the season.

The Night Santa Lost His Magic

Growing up in the old ways of Appalachia, we were taught early on to believe in all sorts of things—ghost stories, old family legends, and, of course, Santa Claus. I was all in on Santa for years, fully convinced that he was out there on Christmas Eve, flying over the mountains to deliver gifts to good kids like me.

But one year, when I was about eight, that all came crashing down. It was Christmas Eve, and I couldn't sleep. The excitement was too much, and I just knew if I stayed up, I'd catch a glimpse of Santa himself. So I crept out of bed and snuck down the hallway, as quiet as I could, hoping to see him coming down our chimney.

Well, instead of Santa, I heard my dad grumbling in the living room. I peeked around the corner and saw him wrestling with a half-built bicycle, muttering under his breath as he tried to attach the handlebars with a screwdriver that clearly wasn't cooperating. I was confused at first—why would Santa leave my dad to do his dirty work? But as I watched, realization dawned. My mom came over with a roll of wrapping paper, and I heard her say, "If he doesn't believe in Santa after this, nothing's gonna convince him."

I was crushed. Not only was Santa not real, but I'd just discovered that my presents were coming from my parents, who apparently weren't magical at all. In fact, they were pretty terrible at assembling bikes!

I tried to sneak back to bed without making a sound, but I think my dad spotted me from the corner of his eye. The next morning, he winked at me as I unwrapped that bike, as if to say, "Welcome to the club, kid." I played along, still pretending to believe for a couple more years, but from then on, I knew the truth.

And to be honest, that Christmas became one of my favorite memories—not because of Santa, but because I got to see my parents, exhausted and laughing, staying up late just to make Christmas magical for us.

The Legendary Christmas Snowball Fight

One Christmas growing up in Stone, Kentucky, we got a snowstorm that was nothing short of legendary. The forecast had predicted just a dusting, maybe an inch or two, but on Christmas Eve, the snow started coming down hard. By Christmas morning, we woke up to over a foot of fresh, powdery snow that blanketed the entire valley, turning our world into a winter wonderland.

After opening our gifts and sharing a warm breakfast, we couldn't resist the call of that snow any longer. We bundled up in every layer we could find—scarves, mismatched gloves, old coats that had been passed down, and boots that didn't quite fit but would do. Then we trudged out into the yard, where our cousins, aunts, and uncles were already gathered, laughing and marveling at the amount of snow that had piled up overnight.

It didn't take long before someone lobbed the first snowball. I still don't know who it was, but that one snowball was all it took to set off an epic, all-out snowball war. Suddenly, the air was filled with flying snowballs, laughter, and the sounds of everyone ducking behind trees and trying to dodge the incoming snow.

My brother and I quickly teamed up and staked out our own little fort by the edge of the barn. We scooped snow as fast as we could, forming a stash of snowballs to defend ourselves. The snow was perfect—light and fluffy but sticky enough to pack into solid, satisfying snowballs. We'd barely built up our stash when we saw a barrage of snowballs flying toward us from across the yard. Our cousins had formed their own "army" and were ready for battle!

We ducked behind our fort, tossing snowballs over the top like we were in some action movie, shouting and whooping as we scored a few hits. But we quickly learned that snowballs travel both ways. My cousin Tommy, who had an arm like a cannon, hit me right in the shoulder, sending snow flying down the back of my neck. It was freezing but hilarious, and I remember laughing so hard I could hardly throw straight.

The battle raged on, moving from the yard to the hillside behind our house. My dad and uncles joined in, chucking snowballs with wild aim and cheering us on. Even my mom, who usually stayed out of these things, got in on the action, ambushing my dad with a well-placed snowball that got him square on the back of the head. We all let out a cheer, and he laughed, shaking off the snow and vowing revenge.

As the afternoon wore on, the snowball fight turned into a massive family-wide game. We formed alliances, made secret snowball stashes, and plotted ambushes, taking cover behind trees and trying to sneak up on each other. The air was filled with squeals of delight and fake battle cries, and every now and then, someone would slip and fall into the snow, only to get pelted by a flurry of snowballs while they tried to get up.

Finally, after hours of fierce (and very cold) competition, we all lay down in the snow, breathless, rosy-cheeked, and exhausted. The snow around us was packed down, a battlefield of footprints, craters, and snow forts. We lay there catching our breath, looking up at the sky, which was already turning that soft pinkish blue as evening started to settle in. The laughter faded into a comfortable quiet, and in that peaceful moment, it felt like the whole world was wrapped in the warmth of family.

That Christmas Day snowball fight is a memory I'll never forget. There was something magical about that snowstorm and the way it brought us all together, turning us back into kids for a few hours. As we tramped back inside, shivering and soaked to the bone, my grandma had hot chocolate waiting for us, along with a reminder to "get those wet clothes off before you catch cold!"

We sipped our hot chocolate with frozen fingers, watching as snowflakes continued to fall outside. It was a Christmas to remember.

A Simple Christmas, A Lifetime of Magic

The first Christmas I can remember as a little girl growing up in Appalachia feels like something out of a storybook, though it was simple by most people's standards. I must've been four or five, young enough that everything seemed so big and magical. I remember waking up to the smell of woodsmoke, with the house feeling extra warm and cozy as snow fell softly outside, blanketing our little corner of the mountains in quiet beauty.

That year, my parents had gone out a few days before to cut down a small pine tree from our land. They hauled it into the house, set it up in the corner of our main room, and we decorated it together. Our decorations were modest, to say the least. We didn't have fancy glass ornaments or glittering lights like you see nowadays. Instead, we strung up popcorn that we'd popped on the stove, and my mom helped me make a few ornaments out of scraps of cloth and old buttons she had saved. I remember how carefully I hung each piece, treating that little tree like it was the grandest Christmas tree in the world. It was beautiful in my eyes, and it felt magical to be part of creating something special.

Christmas Eve was a quiet evening. My parents read the Christmas story from an old, worn Bible by the fire, their voices soft and reverent, and I remember feeling that sense of awe and peace in the stillness of our home. When they finished, my dad gave me a little pat on the head and told me to get to bed, or "Santa might pass us right by." Of course, I hustled off, even though excitement made it hard to sleep. I lay there, watching the shadows from the fire flicker across the walls and wondering what surprises Santa might bring.

Christmas morning came, and I jumped out of bed, running into the main room where the tree was. Underneath, there were a few small gifts, wrapped carefully in plain brown paper tied with bits of twine. My heart nearly burst with excitement. My parents had big smiles on their faces as I knelt down to unwrap each gift slowly, savoring every moment.

One of my gifts that year was a small rag doll my mom had made herself. She'd stitched it together from leftover fabric, with button eyes and yarn hair, and I thought it was the most beautiful doll I'd ever seen. I named her Sally on the spot and spent the rest of the morning introducing her to my other treasures—a wooden whistle my dad had carved for me, a coloring book, and a box of crayons. Those gifts weren't big or expensive, but they felt like treasures to me. Each one was special because I knew the love and care my parents had put into making that Christmas just a little extra special for me.

Later that day, family started arriving. I remember the house filling up with uncles, aunts, and cousins, all of them bringing something to add to the Christmas feast. My mom had been cooking all morning, and the smell of roasting ham and fresh biscuits filled the air. We set up a big, crowded table with every dish you could think of—mashed potatoes, green beans, cornbread, and my aunt's famous apple pie. Us kids sat on little stools or crowded onto laps when chairs ran out, everyone laughing and passing plates around. It was loud and chaotic, but it felt wonderful to be surrounded by the people I loved.

After we'd eaten our fill, my dad took me outside for a walk in the snow. I remember holding his gloved hand as we walked down to the creek, the snow crunching under our feet and the whole world feeling so quiet and pure. We stopped to listen to the water running under the ice, and he pointed out animal tracks, telling me about the deer and raccoons that lived nearby. I remember him lifting me up so I could see the tracks better, my little boots dangling above the snow as he held me close. I felt safe, loved, and so very happy.

That first Christmas memory is so clear in my mind, even all these years later. There wasn't anything fancy about it, no shiny decorations or expensive gifts, but it was filled with love, warmth, and joy. My parents did everything they could to make Christmas feel magical, even in our humble little home in the mountains. They gave me the best gift of all—a sense of wonder, of family, and of simple, lasting happiness.

Now, as I celebrate Christmas with my own children and grandchildren, I find myself bringing some of those traditions back. We make homemade decorations, stringing popcorn for the tree and making ornaments from scraps and buttons, just like I did as a child. We gather close, sharing food, stories, and laughter, and I feel my heart swell, knowing I'm passing on the same sense of love and togetherness that was given to me so long ago.

The Greatest Gift: Keeping Christ in Christmas

Growing up in Prestonsburg, Kentucky, Christmas was always a time of great excitement, filled with traditions, family gatherings, and of course, gifts. But through all the fun and festivities, one thing my parents made sure to remind us year after year was that JESUS IS THE REASON FOR THE SEASON. It wasn't just a saying they passed off with a smile; it was a lesson they wove into every part of our Christmas celebrations, and it stuck with me in a way that has lasted a lifetime.

We didn't have a lot of money growing up. Our house was modest, but it was filled with love, and that love centered around our faith. Christmas was a time to celebrate the birth of Jesus, and my parents made sure we understood that, no matter what gifts we received or how much we loved the twinkling lights on the tree, the real reason we celebrated was because of the miracle that happened in Bethlehem all those years ago.

In the weeks leading up to Christmas, my mom would sit us down after supper, the fire crackling in the hearth, and tell us the story of Jesus' birth. She'd read from the Bible, her voice steady and gentle, and we'd listen intently, the warmth of the fire and her words wrapping around us like a blanket. "This is why we celebrate, children," she'd say, as she'd tell us about Mary and Joseph, the shepherds in the fields, and the wise men who followed the star. "Without Jesus, there would be no Christmas."

Of course, as kids, we were still excited about the tree, the decorations, and the thought of presents under the tree. But my parents didn't let us lose sight of the true meaning. They took us to church every Sunday, and on Christmas Eve, we'd always attend the candlelight service. The church, small but filled with the voices of our community, felt like something sacred, especially on that night. The choir would sing carols, and the pastor would speak of the birth of Christ, reminding everyone, young and old, that Jesus was the greatest gift we'd ever receive.

At home, my father would often lead us in prayer before we sat down to the Christmas meal. His voice, deep and steady, would thank God for the gift of His Son, and for the blessings of family and health. "Remember, children," he'd say as we bowed our heads, "Christmas isn't about what we get, but about what we give, and about what God gave us." My brother and I would glance at each other, our hearts full, even though we were still dreaming about the presents we'd soon be tearing into. But the words stuck, even then.

One of my favorite memories was our family's tradition of putting together a nativity scene. We didn't have one of those fancy sets with porcelain figures; ours was a homemade collection of figurines, hand-carved from wood by my granddad. Each year, we'd pull out the pieces—the stable, the angels, the animals, and the little baby Jesus—and carefully arrange them under the tree. My mom would always make sure the baby Jesus figure was placed in the manger last, and before we did, we'd all gather around and say a prayer. It wasn't the most extravagant nativity set, but it had so much meaning to us. It was a physical reminder that the true meaning of Christmas wasn't wrapped in shiny paper or hidden in a stocking; it was in that humble manger, where Jesus came into the world.

As we got older, there were times when we, like all children, got caught up in the commercial side of Christmas. The world outside seemed to grow more focused on buying and receiving, on "what's under the tree." But every year, my parents would pull us back, reminding us that the best gift we could give wasn't something bought with money—it was the love we shared with others, the kindness we showed, and the gratitude we had for the blessings in our lives.

I remember one Christmas in particular when my brother and I were excited to open the gifts we'd been dreaming about. We'd told Santa exactly what we wanted, and the anticipation was building. But just before we dove into the presents, my mom asked us to stop. She handed us a small box, wrapped in plain brown paper, and inside were several handmade Christmas cards and a few simple toys we'd made ourselves, intended for the families in need in our community. "This," she said softly, "is the true meaning of Christmas. Giving, not just receiving."

We spent the rest of the day delivering those little gifts to neighbors and friends who were struggling. The smiles on their faces, the way they thanked us, taught us something we hadn't quite understood before. Christmas wasn't about the stuff—it was about the spirit of giving, the joy that came from loving others and sharing what we had. That lesson stuck with me far more than any toy ever did. And years later, I understood that my parents were giving us more than material gifts—they were teaching us the values of faith, love, and kindness that would shape who we became.

Now, as an adult, I carry those lessons with me into my own home. Every Christmas, I tell my children the same stories, share the same traditions, and remind them just as my parents reminded me: JESUS IS THE REASON FOR THE SEASON. We hang our nativity scene with the same reverence, we gather around the table with a prayer, and we give to others—because Christmas isn't about what we get; it's about celebrating the birth of Christ and the love we share with the world. And that's a gift that keeps on giving, year after year.

Through Her Eyes: The Magic of Christmas Rediscovered

Christmas always felt like something bigger than just a holiday—it was a season full of wonder, magic, and, for me, a chance to see the world through the wide-eyed excitement of my younger sibling. I was the oldest, so by the time Christmas rolled around each year, I had already been through the routine—helping decorate the tree, writing the letter to Santa, and staying up late to sneak peeks at the gifts hidden under the bed. But watching my younger brother or sister experience it all for the first time? That was something different. It was like rediscovering Christmas all over again, through their innocent awe.

I can still remember the first Christmas when my little sister, Trudy, was old enough to truly understand what was happening. She was maybe five, and the magic of the season was in her eyes every time she looked out the window at the snow falling gently, or when she saw the lights twinkling on the tree. Her excitement was contagious. She would tug at my sleeve, her voice full of wonder, "Do you think Santa's already up in the mountains, bringing toys to all the good boys and girls?" Her belief was pure, and that belief made everything about Christmas feel just a little bit brighter.

One of my favorite memories is of the night we went to cut down our tree. Our family didn't have much money, but we had the land, and every year we'd walk through the snow-covered woods until we found the perfect pine tree to bring inside. It was cold and quiet in the forest, just the crunch of our boots in the snow and the sound of branches swaying in the wind. I remember how my sister's little face lit up when we found the tree, her small hands brushing the snow from the branches, her eyes wide with excitement. She kept saying, "This is the one! This is the one, I can feel it!" Her joy was so infectious, and I couldn't help but feel like we had just discovered something magical—something that only children like her could truly appreciate.

Back home, we decorated the tree together, and every year, I'd let my sister hang the first ornament. She would carefully pick one out, holding it like it was the most precious thing in the world, and hang it on a low branch so she could admire it. The way her face would light up when she stood back to look at the finished tree—it was like she had discovered something new and wonderful. The Christmas lights twinkled, casting a soft glow on the room, and I could see the reflection of the colorful lights in her eyes. For a moment, it felt like time had stopped. I wasn't just the big sister anymore; I was watching her take in something that felt like the most beautiful thing in the world.

On Christmas Eve, my parents would tuck us in with the promise of a visit from Santa. I'd lay there in bed, listening to the sounds of my parents whispering in the kitchen, preparing for the big day. But all I could think about was my little sister, lying in the bed beside me, her tiny face pressed to the pillow, wide-eyed and waiting. She was convinced that if she stayed up long enough, she'd catch a glimpse of Santa, and she'd talk about it endlessly, her voice full of excitement and wonder. "What do you think he looks like? Do you think he wears a red suit even when it's not Christmas?" she'd ask, her words tumbling out in a rush. I'd laugh quietly, trying to ease her to sleep, but part of me wanted to stay up with her and see the world as she did, with all that innocent belief in magic.

And then, on Christmas morning, I'd wake to the sound of her laughter. She'd be the first one up, of course, and when she saw the stockings filled with treats and the presents stacked under the tree, her excitement was pure and uncontainable. She'd jump on my bed, shaking me awake with a grin from ear to ear, practically bouncing as she yelled, "Santa came! He came!" Her joy was so raw, so unfiltered. It wasn't just about the toys or the candy or the treats—it was about the wonder of the season, the belief that something magical had happened in the night. Watching her face light up as she discovered her new doll, or the little wooden toy that my dad had spent hours carving with his own hands, was like seeing Christmas through the eyes of a child for the first time.

I remember how, after the presents were unwrapped, we would sit by the fire and sip hot cocoa, our hands wrapped around the mugs, the warmth spreading through us. My little sister would still be in awe, picking up each gift, her eyes sparkling as she tried to take it all in. She'd thank everyone for their presents, with that same excited, wide-eyed wonder, and I couldn't help but feel grateful for the chance to witness that innocence—the way she still believed in the magic, in the wonder, in the simplicity of Christmas.

Looking back now, as an adult, I realize how much that experience shaped my own love for the Christmas season. There's something powerful about seeing the world through a child's eyes, and something even more special when it's your sibling, someone you've grown up with, discovering the magic for the first time. Christmas wasn't just about the decorations or the gifts; it was about the love, the wonder, and the joy that filled our hearts. And every year, watching my younger sibling experience that joy, I remembered just how beautiful Christmas could be. It wasn't about anything material—it was about family, tradition, and the simple, beautiful belief that something magical could happen when you least expected it.

The Red Truck: A Lesson in True Giving

Christmas was a season full of hope and joy, but it was also a time when the differences between those who had enough and those who didn't could feel especially sharp. I remember one Christmas that stands out in my mind, a Christmas when my parents taught me the true meaning of giving, not just in terms of material gifts, but in giving from the heart.

I was about ten years old, still in elementary school, and like most kids my age, I couldn't wait for Christmas. We were always excited about the presents we'd receive, but we didn't have a lot of money, so the gifts were simple. It was the little things that meant the most—handmade socks or a doll that my mom had sewn from leftover fabric. To me, those gifts were treasures. But as excited as I was, I couldn't help but notice that not all the kids at school shared the same experience.

There was one boy in my class, Johnny, whose family didn't have much. His clothes were always worn, his shoes were patched, and he never seemed to have the same things we did. He didn't come from a bad family; they just didn't have enough to go around. His father worked at the Gary coal mine, just like mine, but the work was often unpredictable, and I knew they struggled to make ends meet. Johnny was quiet and kept to himself, often sitting alone in the cafeteria or playing by himself during recess. I knew he didn't have the kind of Christmas I looked forward to every year.

One day, just before Christmas, our teacher announced a special project: we were going to participate in a gift exchange for less fortunate children. Each of us was asked to bring in a toy or something we thought would make another child smile. The idea was that we would pool our resources together and give something special to a child in need. I was excited, of course, but it also made me stop and think about Johnny. I couldn't help but wonder if he would have a gift at all.

I went home that evening and told my parents about the project. My dad gave me a long look, and my mom nodded. "That's a good thing you're doing, honey," she said. "But maybe there's someone you know who could use a little extra cheer this year." I knew exactly who she meant—Johnny.

I didn't have much to give, but I remembered something. A few weeks earlier, my mom had taken me to the local dollar store, and I'd picked out a little wooden toy truck I thought was the coolest thing. It wasn't much, but it was something I loved. It was bright red with blue wheels, simple but sturdy. I'd been looking forward to playing with it, but now I realized that it could bring joy to someone else, someone who might not have any toys of his own.

That night, I wrapped it up carefully, using some old Christmas paper my mom had saved. I thought about Johnny as I taped the paper down. I could picture him opening it, his eyes lighting up in surprise and maybe even a little bit of wonder. I didn't know if he'd ever gotten a brand-new toy before, but I wanted to make sure this one was special for him.

The next day at school, we all lined up to exchange our gifts. The room was buzzing with excitement as kids passed out presents, and I could see the smiles on their faces as they gave and received. But my heart was focused on one gift: Johnny's. I was so nervous as I handed it to him. He took it from my hands, a little confused at first, like he wasn't sure why I was giving it to him. But when he opened the paper and saw the truck, his face softened. A small smile crept across his face, and I saw the light in his eyes, a kind of quiet joy that made my chest tighten with emotion.

"Thanks," he said softly, and I could tell he wasn't used to being given something like this. His words were simple, but they meant so much. I didn't need any more thanks or recognition. The look on his face was enough to make my heart swell. It wasn't the gift that mattered most—it was knowing I had made a difference, even if just for a moment, in someone else's life.

The rest of the day felt different. The joy of giving stayed with me, warm in my heart. I didn't have much, but I had enough to make sure Johnny had something to smile about that Christmas. It wasn't a big gesture, but it felt important. I didn't expect anything in return, and Johnny didn't need to say anything else. His gratitude was written in the way his eyes lit up when he looked at the truck, and in the quiet way he clutched it to his chest as he sat back down at his desk.

That Christmas taught me something I've carried with me ever since: that the true meaning of giving isn't about how much you have, but how much of yourself you give. The joy I saw in Johnny's eyes was the greatest gift of all. It was a reminder that the holidays aren't just about receiving; they're about making the world a little brighter for someone else. Whether it's a toy, a kind word, or a moment of your time, giving is what makes Christmas special. It's what makes it meaningful.

And in that moment, I realized that the best gift we can give is the one that comes from the heart, the one that shows someone they are seen, they are valued, and they are loved—especially when they least expect it. That's what Christmas is really about.

Stitched with Love: The Gift from My Heart

I remember one Christmas, when I was around 12 years old, that became a turning point for me in understanding the true spirit of giving. It was the year I decided to make my parents a homemade gift, and it's a memory that still fills me with warmth and pride.

The holiday season in our small mountain town was always magical. Snow would fall gently, covering the hillsides in a blanket of white, and the scent of wood smoke filled the air. Our house was small, nestled in a valley with the sound of the creek nearby, and inside, there was always a fire crackling in the stove. We didn't have much in the way of decorations or fancy gifts, but my mom always made our home feel festive. She'd pull out old ornaments from the box in the attic, the ones that had been passed down through generations, and we'd hang them on our little tree. Each one told a story, each one held a memory.

That year, as Christmas approached, I started thinking about what I could give my parents. The thought of buying something seemed impossible—there simply wasn't enough money for extras like that. But I didn't want to give up on giving them something special. I wanted to make something with my own hands, something that would show them how much I appreciated everything they'd done for me.

I remember sitting at the kitchen table one evening, my fingers tapping on the old wooden surface, thinking about what I could make. My eyes landed on the scraps of fabric that were always piled up in the corner. My mom had a sewing machine, and she'd taught me to sew over the years, so I knew my way around a needle and thread. I thought about it for a while and then had an idea—why not make them something that could both serve a purpose and carry a piece of me with it? A quilt.

It wasn't a big quilt, not the kind you'd see in stores, but something simple and heartfelt. My mother had always loved quilts, and I remembered the one she had growing up—worn but beautiful, a patchwork of colorful pieces that had been lovingly sewn together. So, I decided to make her a quilt for Christmas—a small one, just big enough to cover the couch where she often sat to read or knit by the fire.

I didn't have much fabric to work with, but that didn't stop me. I scrounged through the old clothes we no longer wore and pulled out pieces of flannel, denim, and cotton. I even used some of the worn-out shirts that my dad no longer wore—ones he'd worked in until the sleeves were frayed. Every piece of fabric had a story. The plaid from my dad's work shirt reminded me of his long hours at the Bonny Blue coal mine. The floral print from an old dress of my mom's made me think of the times she'd worked hard to make our house a home, always putting others before herself. The fabrics were simple, but each one was woven with memories, and it felt like I was stitching together pieces of our life.

I spent the next few weeks working on the quilt, taking my time to cut the fabric into squares, carefully stitching them together. My fingers ached from pushing the needle through thick layers of fabric, but each stitch felt like an act of love. I worked late into the night, the hum of the sewing machine keeping me company. The whole time, I thought about my parents—the sacrifices they made, the long days they worked to make sure we had enough, the love they showed every day, even when things were hard.

I'll never forget the day I finished the quilt. It was just a few days before Christmas, and I put the final stitches in place, tying off the ends. The quilt wasn't perfect—it had a few uneven seams and the corners didn't line up exactly the way I wanted—but it didn't matter. What mattered was the love and time I had put into it. As I spread it out on the couch to admire it, I felt a sense of pride and accomplishment. This was something that came from my heart, something that said "I love you" without words.

Christmas morning came, and the excitement was palpable. My little brother and sister were already up, excitedly unwrapping their gifts. I watched as they tore through their presents, their laughter filling the house. But I knew that my gift for my parents was the one I was most excited about. After breakfast, when we were all gathered around the tree, I handed them the quilt, wrapped up in simple brown paper and tied with twine.

They both looked at it, their eyes wide with surprise. I remember my mom's face softening as she gently unwrapped it. When she saw the quilt, her eyes filled with tears, and she pulled me into a tight hug. My dad's voice cracked when he spoke, "This is the most beautiful gift, honey. Thank you."

I hadn't expected that reaction. I had expected them to appreciate it, but seeing their emotions, seeing how much it meant to them, made all the hours of work and the effort worth it. The quilt wasn't fancy, it wasn't new, but it was a symbol of my love for them, and that was all that mattered.

That Christmas, I learned something I've carried with me ever since. It's not the cost of the gift or the grandeur of the wrapping paper that makes Christmas special—it's the thought, the time, and the love you put into it. It's about giving something of yourself, something that comes from the heart. The quilt wasn't perfect, but it was made with all the love and gratitude I could give, and that's what made it truly special.

As the years have passed, I've carried on that tradition of homemade gifts, and I always think back to that Christmas when I made my parents that quilt. Every time I create something with my own hands, I remember that feeling of love and joy I saw in their eyes, and I know that giving from the heart is the most meaningful gift of all.

The Heart of a Simple Christmas

Christmas has changed so much since the days I was growing up in the hills of Maggie Valley, North Carolina. When I look back on those memories, I feel a mix of nostalgia and wonder, realizing just how different the holiday season has become. Growing up, Christmas wasn't about lavish gifts, fancy decorations, or the latest technology. It was about togetherness, simplicity, and finding joy in the little things—things that seem to have faded into the background of Christmas today.

Back then, Christmas was about the buildup, the little traditions that made the whole season feel magical. We'd start counting down the days to Christmas with a paper chain my mom would help us make, each link representing one day closer to the holiday. Each night before bed, we'd excitedly rip off one link, feeling the excitement grow as the chain got shorter. Now, it feels like there are countdown apps and calendars with chocolates or little gifts for every day in December, but they lack that homemade charm. Back then, our excitement came from simple things, things we made and treasured ourselves.

Decorating was another part of Christmas that feels so different now. We didn't have yards full of blow-up Santas or lights synchronized to music. Our decorations were modest but meaningful. We'd go out into the woods as a family, searching for a Christmas tree that we could cut down ourselves. There was something magical about walking through the forest in the chill of December, bundled up in our coats and mittens, each of us scanning the trees to find "the one." Sometimes it was small and a bit lopsided, but it was ours, and bringing it home felt like bringing a piece of the wilderness into our living room.

Our tree was decorated with what we had—no fancy store-bought ornaments or color-coordinated themes. We'd string popcorn and cranberries for garlands, making it a family affair as we laughed and told stories while our fingers grew sticky from the cranberries. Our ornaments were often handmade or passed down, each one with a story behind it. My favorite was a little angel made of cornhusks, crafted by my grandmother. Hanging it on the tree each year felt like a way to honor her and all the love she put into our family. Today, it feels like decorations are all about style and trends, but back then, every piece had meaning.

Gift-giving was another thing entirely. Growing up, none of us expected big gifts, and we certainly didn't make long lists of items we wanted. Times were tight, and my parents taught us to appreciate the thought behind each present. I remember one year when my mom knitted us each a new pair of mittens and hats. We didn't see them as small gifts or wish for more; we saw them as precious because we knew she had spent hours making them just for us. Another year, my dad whittled a wooden toy horse for me, painting it with leftover paint he'd found in the shed. I can still remember the pride in his eyes when he handed it to me. It wasn't about the size or price of the gift; it was about the love that went into it.

These days, it feels like Christmas is all about the newest gadgets, long wish lists, and the pressure to get more, do more, and spend more. I walk into stores and see aisles full of toys and electronics, all wrapped up in plastic and glitter, but I wonder how many of them will still be loved a few years from now. Growing up, we cherished the few gifts we received. They were treasures because they came from the heart and because they were so thoughtfully made or chosen.

Our Christmas meals were a reflection of our Appalachian roots as well. We didn't have a huge spread or a fancy feast. We'd have simple dishes, most of them cooked from scratch using what we had at home. My mom would make a ham, sometimes a turkey if we'd had a good year, and we'd have green beans we'd canned in the summer, sweet potatoes, and fresh biscuits. Dessert was usually my favorite part—she'd make an apple pie or a stack cake with layers of homemade applesauce, a recipe that had been in our family for generations. We'd sit around the table, grateful for the food we shared, knowing that it had taken hard work and love to bring it all together.

Now, it seems like Christmas meals are all about excess. Buffets of food, table settings that look like they belong in a magazine, and so many choices that it's hard to even appreciate them all. Back then, every dish was special because it was made with love, and we savored every bite. We were grateful for what we had, and I think that gratitude was what made everything taste so much sweeter.

And then there was the sense of community, the feeling that Christmas wasn't just a day for family but a time for neighbors and friends, too. We'd bundle up and go caroling through the neighborhood, our voices ringing out into the quiet night. People would open their doors, smiling, sometimes inviting us in for hot cocoa or a slice of cake. Church was the center of the season, too, with a Christmas Eve service that everyone attended. We'd dress in our Sunday best, holding candles as we sang hymns and listened to the story of Jesus's birth. That feeling of togetherness, of being connected to something bigger than ourselves, was what made Christmas feel so special.

Now, it feels like so much of that has faded. People seem more focused on the busyness of shopping and decorating, and less on simply being together. Christmas has become a whirlwind of tasks and checklists, but growing up, it was slow, intentional, and rooted in tradition. We didn't have much, but we had each other, and that was more than enough. Looking back, I realize how blessed I was to grow up with those simple Christmases.

A Christmas Wrapped in Scarves and Love

I'll never forget the Christmas when my mom sat me down by the fireplace and told me the story of a Christmas she had growing up in Appalachia—a Christmas with no presents. I must have been eight or nine at the time, and I remember thinking how strange that sounded. To me, Christmas was all about the wonder of gifts under the tree, the excitement of unwrapping surprises. But as I listened to her story, I felt my heart soften and my understanding of Christmas change forever.

Mom grew up in the small coal town of Red Jacket, West Virginia, where money was always tight and times were often hard. Her parents had migrated to the coalfields from Italy and started in this country from scratch. Her family was large, with seven children all packed into a modest home with drafty windows and creaky floors. Her dad worked long hours in the mines, and her mom took on any work she could find, from mending clothes for neighbors to baking pies to sell at the local market. They didn't have much, but they had each other, and that was what held them together.

One year, when my mom was just a girl, things were especially hard. My grandpa had fallen ill, which meant they had even less money coming in. My grandma worked herself to the bone, doing whatever she could to keep food on the table and keep the house warm. But as Christmas drew near, it became clear that there just wasn't going to be enough left over for presents.

My mom told me that she had been hopeful right up until Christmas Eve. She remembered standing by the window, looking out at the quiet night, and wishing with all her might that somehow, someway, a present might appear. But when Christmas morning came, there were no gifts under the tree. There was no money for a new doll, no pretty dress, not even a little toy horse, which was all she had really wanted that year.

Instead, her mom gathered the children around and explained that Christmas wasn't about what was under the tree; it was about the love they had for each other and the simple gift of being together. My mom said that her mother's words were so gentle, so full of warmth, that even though she was disappointed, she felt comforted. Grandma handed each of them a small hand-knitted scarf she'd made from yarn scraps, each one a different color. They weren't fancy, but each scarf was made with love, each stitch woven with care and thought. She'd worked late at night, long after the children had gone to bed, her fingers sore from the hours of knitting in the candlelight.

When she handed them their scarves, she told them that Christmas was about giving, and while they might not have much in the way of material things, they had love, and that was the greatest gift anyone could ask for. She told them that love was something no one could take from them, and that as long as they kept love alive in their hearts, they would always be rich. My mom's siblings, though they were young, seemed to understand. They wore their scarves proudly, as if they'd been given the finest gifts in the world.

Then Grandma pulled out her old Bible and read them the Christmas story, telling them how Mary and Joseph had no room at the inn, how they made do in a stable and welcomed the greatest gift of all into the world, surrounded by nothing more than hay and animals. My mom said that hearing that story put things into perspective for her, even as a little girl. It helped her realize that Christmas wasn't about how much you had, but how much you loved and appreciated the things you did have.

That Christmas morning, my mom and her brothers and sisters bundled up in their scarves and headed outside, playing in the snow and building little forts along the hillside. They made up games, laughing and cheering as they threw snowballs, all the while feeling the warmth of their mother's love wrapped around them in the form of those handmade scarves. When they went back inside, their mother had made a simple meal, and they all sat around their small table, holding hands and giving thanks for each other. They didn't have fancy dishes or a feast, but they had warmth, and they had each other.

As my mom told me this story, I remember looking at her and seeing a softness in her eyes, like she was looking back through a window into her childhood. I could tell how much that Christmas meant to her, even though there were no gifts. In a way, it had been the most meaningful Christmas she'd ever had. She told me that from that day forward, she understood that Christmas was about togetherness and the spirit of giving, even if all you had to give was something as simple as a handmade scarf.

The Season of Waiting: A Childhood Christmas Countdown

Growing up in Appalachia, the anticipation of Christmas was one of the most magical parts of the entire season. Looking back, it feels like the days between Thanksgiving and Christmas stretched on forever, with each passing day filled with a mix of wonder, excitement, and the quiet beauty of our simple traditions. The holiday season had a slower rhythm back then, one that allowed the anticipation to build naturally. There was something special about that waiting, something that made Christmas feel like more than just a single day. It was a whole season of little joys, quiet traditions, and the sense that something wonderful was coming.

It all started with the first frost. That first chilly morning, when you'd wake up to find the ground covered in a shimmering layer of frost, meant that Christmas was on its way. We'd pull on our boots and run outside, leaving little footprints in the frosted grass, our breath puffing out in clouds. There was a thrill in that first chill of winter air, a promise of snow to come and the magic of Christmas waiting just around the corner.

Then there was the ritual of making a paper chain, a long strip of red and green paper links that would hang in our living room. Every evening, my siblings and I would tear off one link, counting down the days until Christmas. Each link felt like a tiny milestone, and the chain grew shorter and shorter as our excitement grew. Tearing off that last link on Christmas Eve was like the grand finale, the moment we'd been waiting for all month. It was a simple tradition, but in a small town without endless activities and decorations, it was enough to fill our hearts with the thrill of what was to come.

We didn't have big shopping malls or online wish lists. Our anticipation wasn't built around endless commercials or advertisements, but around the small traditions we shared as a family. One of my favorite traditions was when my mom would gather us around to help bake Christmas cookies. She'd make the dough from scratch, rolling it out on the kitchen table, and we'd use our old tin cookie cutters to press out shapes—stars, bells, and little Christmas trees. We'd sprinkle them with colored sugar and place them carefully on the baking sheets. The smell of cookies baking would fill the whole house, and even as we tried to sneak bites of raw dough, our minds were already racing ahead to Christmas morning.

Another favorite ritual was decorating the house with whatever we had on hand. We didn't have elaborate Christmas lights or store-bought garlands, but that didn't matter. We'd gather pine branches from the woods and arrange them on the mantle, adding a few homemade ornaments. Sometimes, we'd string popcorn and cranberries into garlands, and I remember pricking my fingers more times than I could count, but the end result was always worth it. There was a quiet pride in seeing our own handiwork on display, knowing that we'd made something beautiful from what we had around us.

And then, of course, there was the anticipation of snow. We didn't always have a white Christmas, but that didn't stop us from wishing for it each year. Every night before bed, we'd peek outside, hoping to see snowflakes starting to fall. On the mornings when we woke up to a world transformed by snow, it felt like a little piece of Christmas magic had arrived early. We'd bundle up and rush outside to play, making snow angels and building forts until our fingers and toes were frozen. Even though we knew it was still days until Christmas, the snow made it feel like the holiday had already begun.

As Christmas Eve approached, the anticipation reached a fever pitch. Our little country church would hold its Christmas Eve service, and we'd dress in our Sunday best, bundling up in scarves and hats against the cold. The church was small and simple, but on Christmas Eve it felt like the most beautiful place in the world. We'd sing carols by candlelight, our voices filling the little sanctuary, and I remember feeling a sense of peace and wonder that I could never quite put into words. Hearing the Christmas story read aloud made everything feel more real, as though we were stepping into something timeless and sacred.

When we got home, my mom would let us open one small gift, usually something practical like socks or mittens she'd knitted herself. We'd unwrap it carefully, savoring the moment, even though it wasn't a toy or a game. It was a way of stretching out the excitement, of taking a little taste of Christmas without jumping right into the big day. We'd hang our stockings, knowing that Santa would fill them overnight, and we'd head to bed with our hearts pounding, wondering what surprises the morning would bring.

Falling asleep on Christmas Eve was its own kind of magic. The house would be quiet, with just the faint glow of the Christmas tree lights casting a soft warmth across the room. I'd lie awake, staring at the ceiling, listening to the creaks of the house and the sounds of the night, wondering if I'd hear Santa's sleigh on the roof. The anticipation was almost too much to bear, a mix of excitement and happiness that made my chest feel tight. I'd close my eyes, imagining the tree piled high with gifts, and drift off into dreams filled with sugarplums and snowflakes.

Christmas morning was always worth the wait. Waking up and rushing to the tree, finding the gifts waiting for us, feeling the warmth of our family around us—those were the moments that made all the anticipation worthwhile. The waiting, the hoping, the quiet little traditions—it all built up to that beautiful, joyful morning when everything felt right in the world.

The Christmas the World Stood Still

One Christmas stands out in my memory—a Christmas when the snow fell so thick and heavy that it felt like the whole world was wrapped in a white, silent blanket. Our little family was tucked into our tiny house on the mountainside, isolated by the snowfall, surrounded by nothing but trees, snowdrifts, and the quiet hush that comes when the world gets buried in winter.

That Christmas Eve, the snow started falling early in the afternoon. I remember watching from the window, the flakes soft and steady, each one adding to the thick carpet of snow on the ground. Daddy went outside to bring in extra firewood, his boots making deep impressions as he shuffled through the drifts. He loaded up the porch, telling Mama with a smile, "Best be prepared—looks like it'll be a big one."

By dusk, the snow was coming down in sheets. The wind howled around the corners of our little house, rattling the windowpanes and making the old boards creak. Mama told us to bundle up, so we gathered around the fireplace, the warmest spot in the house, pulling quilts and blankets around our shoulders.

As the night wore on, we lost power. The whole valley went dark, and the only light we had was from the glow of the fireplace and the little oil lamps Mama lit and set around the room. We sat in the soft glow, watching the fire dance and listening to the storm. Daddy closed the shutters and stuffed blankets in any cracks to keep out the draft, and before long, our whole world was reduced to the tiny, cozy space we shared around that hearth.

That night, Mama pulled out her Bible and read us the Christmas story, her voice soft and steady, telling us about that little stable far away and the star that shone down on that holy night. I remember how her words mingled with the wind outside, like they were both part of the same ancient, timeless story. There was something beautiful about sitting there together in the quiet, away from everything, surrounded by nothing but snow.

When we woke up Christmas morning, the world outside was still blanketed in white. Snowdrifts covered the front door, and the windows were frosted over. We could barely see outside. Daddy tried to open the door but could only get it open a few inches. "Looks like we're snowed in," he said with a laugh, his breath making little puffs in the cold air.

Instead of presents under the tree that year, we had each other. Mama rummaged around the kitchen and pulled out a few ingredients she'd been saving for Christmas morning—some flour, a little molasses, and a jar of apple preserves she'd canned in the fall. She mixed up the ingredients and made a batch of cookies. We sat around watching her roll out the dough on the counter, shaping each cookie by hand. She even let us cut a few into star shapes, telling us, "Every Christmas deserves a little starlight, even if it's made from dough."

Daddy stoked the fire, and we baked those cookies right there on the hearth, filling the room with the sweet, spicy smell. It was simple, but it felt magical, like we were sharing in something special, something just for us.

When we'd finished, Daddy took out his old harmonica and played us some carols. He wasn't much of a musician, but he put his heart into it, and we sang along, our voices filling the little house. "Silent Night," "Hark the Herald Angels Sing," and "O Holy Night." There was no grand piano, no choir—just a harmonica, a fire, and the sound of our voices echoing off the walls.

After our "concert," Mama brought out a jar of homemade apple butter, and we spread it on slices of bread she'd baked a few days earlier. Sitting around in that quiet house, munching on bread and apple butter, it felt like we had all the riches in the world.

As the day wore on, the snow outside began to ease up, but it was clear we weren't going anywhere anytime soon. Daddy went to the back room and brought out a surprise—a set of carved wooden toys he'd made for each of us. He'd spent weeks working on them in the evenings when we were asleep, sanding down the wood until it was smooth, carving details into each little figure. For my brother, he'd made a little wooden car. For me, there was a doll with a painted-on smile and little corn-husk hair. Holding that doll in my hands, I felt like I'd been given the most precious gift in the world.

We spent the rest of that Christmas day playing with our toys, listening to stories by the fire, and just soaking up the warmth of being together. There were no presents wrapped in fancy paper, no feast on the table, no big tree adorned with glittering lights. But there was laughter, and there was love, and the quiet peace that only comes when you're surrounded by the people who matter most.

I look back on that Christmas now with so much fondness. We had so little, but in some ways, it felt like we had everything. That simple Christmas, snowed in and snuggled together in our tiny home, taught me that sometimes the most magical things in life are the simplest ones. It wasn't about what we had or didn't have; it was about the love that filled our home, the warmth that radiated from our little fire, and the quiet joy of knowing we were safe, together, and loved.

From Bare Branches to Bright Lights: A Legacy of Christmas Love

Christmases were simple and sometimes tough. The hollers and mountain towns I grew up in were beautiful places, but work wasn't always steady, and most families, including mine, struggled just to make ends meet. Even though my parents did everything they could to make the season feel special, there were years when Christmas was about as bare as the trees outside. My siblings and I knew that some years there'd be only a small, shared gift or two under the tree, and we'd do our best to focus on the joy of being together. But even as a kid, I promised myself that one day, if I had a family, I'd do everything I could to give my kids a good Christmas.

Now, as an adult, there's no better feeling than seeing my children's faces light up on Christmas morning. It's hard to describe the pride I feel knowing I've been able to give them a Christmas I once only dreamed of. I know, from experience, that Christmas isn't just about presents, but I also know what it feels like to wish for something special and not have it. That's why, each year, I do my best to make Christmas magical for them.

In the weeks leading up to the big day, I start planning and saving wherever I can. I'll hunt for deals, put a little extra aside from every paycheck, and do whatever it takes to make sure the holiday season is as bright as it can be. There's a satisfaction in stretching every dollar, knowing that each bit I save is going to make their Christmas a little brighter. I remember the times when my own parents scraped together whatever they could to put something special under the tree, even if it was small. Now that I'm the one holding up that tradition, I understand the sacrifices they made and the pride they must've felt too, knowing they did everything they could to bring some joy into our lives.

As a parent, there's something incredibly fulfilling about setting up the tree with my kids, watching their excitement as they hang the ornaments and place the star on top. We always take a step back to admire our handiwork, and in those moments, I'm filled with a pride that runs deep. I see their joy, and I'm grateful that I can give them something I know they'll remember for years to come. It's not about lavish gifts or going overboard, but about creating a sense of wonder and comfort, a memory of Christmas that will stay with them, just like my own Christmas memories have stayed with me.

Christmas Eve, once the kids are in bed, my wife and I sneak around, arranging the gifts, filling the stockings, and adding any final touches. There's a deep sense of satisfaction as I lay each gift under the tree, knowing I've kept my promise to myself, that I'm able to give my kids what I couldn't always have. It's in those quiet moments, with the twinkle of the lights and the stillness of the house, that I feel the weight of the journey we've come through. The early days of struggling to make ends meet, to find a steady job, to build a life that was better than what I'd known growing up—all those challenges feel worth it in that moment.

When Christmas morning finally comes, and the kids rush into the room, their eyes wide with wonder, all the hard work and planning pays off. Their laughter fills the house as they tear into the wrapping paper, each gift bringing more excitement than the last. It's not just the presents, but the entire spirit of the season that fills our home with joy and warmth. And I know that I've done right by them, that I've given them something special, something I once longed for myself.

But beyond the gifts and the decorations, what means the most to me is the security, warmth, and togetherness that I can offer. I want them to feel safe and loved, to know that we're here for each other, no matter what. I'm proud to provide not just the things they'll open on Christmas morning, but the sense of stability and love that I worked so hard to create.

Christmas is a time to celebrate, but it's also a time to reflect. As I watch my kids, I think about my own parents and the sacrifices they made for us, even when there was so little to go around. They taught me that Christmas isn't just about the gifts under the tree, but about the strength of family, the power of love, and the pride in giving whatever you can to make your family feel special. Now, as a parent myself, I understand that more than ever, and I feel grateful to be able to carry on that legacy in my own way.

In the end, Christmas is more than one day, more than presents or traditions. It's a season of giving, of gratitude, and of love. And I'm filled with pride knowing that, despite the challenges I faced growing up, I've built a life where I can give my kids the Christmas I always dreamed of—a Christmas where they feel loved, secure, and filled with joy. And that, to me, is the greatest gift of all.

Made in the USA
Columbia, SC
29 November 2024

47868027R10039